Competition and Regulation in Telecommunications

Examining Germany and America

AF787959

Competition and Regulation in Telecommunications

Examining Germany and America

edited by

J. Gregory Sidak
American Enterprise Institute
for Public Policy Research

Christoph Engel
University of Osnabrück

Günter Knieps
University of Freiburg

Springer Science+Business Media, LLC

Library of Congress Cataloging-in-Publication Data

Competition and regulation in telecommunications : examining Germany and America / edited by J. Gregory Sidak, Christoph Engel, Günter Knieps.
p. cm.
Includes bibliographical references and index.
Contents: Tangled telecommunications regulation / Wernhard Möschel -- The path to competition for telecommunications in Germany / Christoph Engel -- Costing and Pricing in liberalized telecommunications markets / Günter Knieps -- Regulation by TSLRIC : economic effects on investment and innovation / Jerry A. Hausman -- What is wrong with American telecommunications? / J. Gregory Sidak, Paul W. MacAvoy.

ISBN 978-94-010-3873-7 ISBN 978-94-010-0640-8 (eBook)
DOI 10.1007/978-94-010-0640-8

1. Telecommunication policy--Germany. 2. Telecommunication policy--United States. I. Sidak, J. Gregory. II. Engel, Christoph, 1956- III. Knieps, Günter.

HE8155 .C66 2000
384'.0943--dc21 00-062478

Copyright © 2001 Springer Science+Business Media New York
Originally published by Kluwer Academic Publishers. in 2001
Softcover reprint of the hardcover 1st edition 2001

All rights reserved. No part of this publication may be reproduced, stored in a retrieval system or transmitted in any form or by any means, mechanical, photocopying, recording, or otherwise, without the prior written permission of the publisher, Springer Science+Business Media, LLC

Printed on acid-free paper.

TABLE OF CONTENTS

CONTRIBUTORS

Christoph Engel directs the Max-Planck-Project Group on the Law of Common Goods at Bonn and is professor of law at the University of Osnabrück.

Jerry A. Hausman is the John and Jennie S. MacDonald Professor of Economics at the Massachusetts Institute of Technology.

Günter Knieps directs the Institute of Transport Economics and Regional Policy and is professor of economics at the University of Freiburg.

Paul W. MacAvoy is the Williams Brothers Professor of Management Studies at the Yale School of Management.

Wernhard Möschel is chairman of the Monopoly Commission of Germany and is professor of law at the University of Tübingen.

J. Gregory Sidak is the F. K. Weyerhaeuser Fellow in Law and Economics at the American Enterprise Institute for Public Policy Research.

FOREWORD

This volume brings together academic economists and lawyers to evaluate and compare the regulation of telecommunications markets in Germany and the United States. The unifying theme in all of the papers is that the goal of public policy in this area should be to make the broadest and most functional competition possible by means of an appropriate regulatory framework. Because the European and American telecommunications markets are becoming more intertwined each day, the issues addressed in this volume will be topical to the business, government, and academic communities for some time.

For the chairman of the Monopoly Commission, Wernhard Möschel, the opening of the German telecommunications market has been successful in principle. This is clearly recognizable in the case of the competition in long-distance transport. Based on the view that the regulatory authority should make itself obsolete, Professor Möschel advocates an incremental review and gradual reduction of regulation. Professors Christoph Engel of the Max-Planck-Project Group on the Law of Collective Property, and Günter Knieps, Director of the Institute of Transport Economics and Regional Policy at Albert Ludwigs-Universität Freiburg, emphasizes that Germany's Telecommunications Act provides not only for service competition in the Deutsche Telekom networks, but also for network competition. According to them, asymmetrical regulation carries with it the risk of the subsidization of inefficient competitors and technologies. They argue that the regulatory goal of "infrastructure competition" is frustrated by regulated interconnections below cost. Asymmetrical regulatory directives that unilaterally hinder infrastructure competition create the wrong incentives on a long-term basis. According to Professors Engel and Knieps, the goal must be specifically to create incentives for infrastructure investments by market newcomers.

J. Gregory Sidak of the American Enterprise Institute, Paul W. MacAvoy of Yale University, and Professor Jerry A. Hausman of the Massachusetts Institute of Technology note the dangers of aberrant economic policy developments as a result of incorrect regulatory decisions. According to them, access by competitors to portions of the network requires that these companies share appropriately in the investment risks of the network operator. In addition, Mr. Sidak and Professors MacAvoy and Hausman argue that unbundling directives should be limited to truly "essential facilities." Otherwise, they reason, new providers will lack the incentive to invest in the construction of their own networks.

The publication of these papers will make important research accessible to a broad audience on both sides of the Atlantic, enrich the public discussion, and thereby contribute to the continuing development of public policy in the dynamic area of telecommunications.

J. GREGORY SIDAK
CHRISTOPH ENGEL
GÜNTER KNIEPS

1

TANGLED TELECOMMUNICATIONS REGULATION

Wernhard Möschel
Monopoly Commission of Germany
University of Tübingen

According to a classic Jewish joke, sweet lemonade is the best contraception of all: not before and not after, but instead of. A similarly effective magic potion is still being sought for the telecommunications sector, in order to draw clear demarcation lines between regulatory responsibilities in place of today's often fuzzy ones. At issue is the relationship between the Regulatory Authority for Telecommunications and Posts and the Federal Cartel Office. Whether the Cartel Office, in substance, applies the German Law against Restraints of Competition (GWB) or the competition rules of the European Union can make a difference. At issue is the position of the Commission in Brussels, the Commission being able to take both legislative and administrative action. And lastly, at issue also is the scope for intervention of the Federal Economics Minister. Is the Telecommunications Regulatory Authority—a higher federal authority in the portfolio of the Economics Ministry—subject to instructions in its individual rulings or can it invoke a certain independence? Or would a way round these issues even be to create a European regulator? Any attempt to mark off limits would be incomplete without mentioning finally that, should the boundaries between telecommunications services according to Section 3 of the German Telecommunications Act (TKG) on the one hand and teleservices or broadcasting according to the Teleservices Act and the Agreement on Media Services between the German Federal States on the other become blurred as a result of the growing convergence trends, the result could be disputed responsibilities with the media authorities in the federal states. This is why Kurt Biedenkopf is assuming only a limited lifetime for the Regulatory Authority, until market forces take care of competition.[1]

I. REGULATORY AUTHORITY AND CARTEL OFFICE

Conflicts of competence between the Regulatory Authority and the Cartel Office can only arise in general areas of overlap such as the control of anticompetitive practices in relation to dominant companies, and not on specific issues like licensing or number management. Here, Section 2(3) of the TKG says nothing more than: "The provisions of the Law against Restraints of Competition shall remain unaffected." This is the wording typically found when laws are to apply in parallel. The substantiation for this provision is more illuminating, however: "This provision sets in context the sector-specific supervision of practices in telecommunications, set forth in a special law, in relation to general competition law and in particular, the Law against Restraints of Competition, which applies on a subsidiary basis whenever no special arrangements are made."[2] Without engaging in argument about objective or subjective methods of interpretation, the legislative intent is clear: there is to be a special relationship between the two laws.[3] And this accords with how they are applied. Concerning the most important issues, this means:

- The TKG provides for rates regulation for a dominant provider's telecommunications services. Rates are regulated on both an ex ante and an ex post basis. Price levels are not controlled by the Federal Cartel Office, the rationale for which would be given by Section 19 of the GWB.

- Priority is also given to the special control of anticompetitive practices as set forth in Section 33 of the TKG (non-discriminatory network access) and consequently the ruling of Section 37 of the TKG concerning the interconnection requirement on public telecommunications carriers. This ruling, however, relates solely to horizontal restrictive practices ("in relation to competitors"). Hence it falls to the Cartel Office to address vertical cases by default, so to speak. Thus the Cartel Office rightly affirmed its jurisdiction for matters relating to Deutsche Telekom/media authority Berlin-Brandenburg when Telekom, as the operator of the broadband cable network in Berlin, refused to give programme providers two additional channels for analogue programmes from the so-called hyperband.[4]

II. CARTEL OFFICE RESPONSIBILITIES UNDER SECTION 50 OF THE GWB

It is not clear whether the Federal Cartel Office would also be prevented from taking action on an issue which fell under the remit of the Regulatory Authority when it was an issue on which the Cartel Office—invoking the empowerment provided by Section 50 (1) of the GWB—was seeking to apply European competition law. The TKG says nothing on this, although the legislators must have been aware of the problem. Certainly, the Mestmäcker/Witte report of November 1995, compiled for the then Posts and Telecommunications Minister, addresses the issue.[5] If Section 50 of the GWB is applied, the idea of specialty in the application of the TKG is stymied, taken almost to the point of adsurdity. Hence it would appear that this provision was also eliminated by tacit agreement, provided that the interventionary powers of the regulator were wide enough. But this must be set against the fact that in Germany, substantive Community law, competition rules included, applies unchanged. The Federal Cartel Office, should it become active under Section 50 of the GWB, is merely a decentralised enforcement body below the level of the European Commission. Crucial is the efficient application of substantive law. This latter consideration, in my view, taking as it does the substance and less the form as its orientation, that is to say the authority for enforcement, appears weightier. Accordingly, Section 50 of the GWB would not be made invalid by the TKG. A similar situation prevailed in the energy industry in the past. The provisions of the Act, notably the prohibition on cartels, were largely overriden. Meanwhile, the Cartel Office, via Section 50, applies the European competition rules.

III. THE RESPONSIBILITIES OF BRUSSELS

Also implied in the above is an assessment of the relationship between the Regulatory Authority and the European Commission in Brussels. Community law retains primacy.[6] And primacy includes the Commission's current administrative responsibilities. Likewise unaffected are the subjective rights of private entities deriving from Article 81 et s. of the EC Treaty, which may be asserted before the courts independently of the Regulatory Authority. These are rights which stem from a similar constitutional basis and which are beyond the control of national legislators. To the extent that the Commission does not intervene in deference to the existing national authorities, we effectively encounter the phenomenon of a division of labour not given in law.[7] In simple terms this means a case can fall under the concurrent jurisdiction of the Regulatory Authority under the TKG, of the Federal Cartel Office via Section 50 of the GWB and of the European Commission in accordance with Community law. In the event of conflict, the Commission will be the one to act. Let me just add two points of detail from substantive law at this stage:

- Each disparate mix of private-law and regulatory action, such as is typically found in the telecommunications sector—for example rates regulation under Sections 24 et s. of the TKG—poses tricky questions about the application of Article 82 of the EC Treaty. To the extent that undertakings have decision-making scope, they are addressed by the ruling. That is in order when a filing is made for rates which are anticompetitively high. Approval by the Regulatory Authority and the ensuing obligation to ask only prices that have been approved, changes nothing.[8] Intervention by the Commission—and also by the Cartel Office via Section 50 of the GWB—against a dominant company's approved pricing is possible on this basis. Examples are the—not few—instances in which the Cartel Office still considered an approved tariff too high.

- When Member States take action with regard to public undertakings according to Article 86(1) in conjunction with Article 82 of the EC Treaty the requirement of accessoriness can be dropped, according to the case law of the European Court of Justice. Such an undertaking need not have its own independent scope of action and be able to eliminate an anticompetitive practice by virtue of its own decisions.[9] With a direct and indirect (via the *Kreditanstalt für Wiederaufbau*, or Reconstruction Loan Corporation) federal government holding of around 74%, Deutsche Telekom AG is a public undertaking within this meaning—critical here is the ability of the government to exercise a controlling influence[10]—price regulation by the Regulatory Authority is at any rate subject to this form of control. Under Article 86(3) of the EC Treaty the Commission can address decisions to the Member State. However, there can be no jurisdiction for the Cartel Office following this line of argument.

IV. FEDERAL ECONOMICS MINISTRY AND REGULATORY AUTHORITY

The relationship between the Federal Economics Ministry and the Regulatory Authority is concerned with whether the Regulatory Authority, in its individual rulings, is subject to instructions from the Ministry. On this, the TKG has largely followed what the GWB says: decisions are to be made by Ruling Chambers, each of which has three members, and there is to be scope for the Minister to issue *general* instructions that will be subject to publication. The independence of the Cartel Office has always been a matter of dispute, just as that of the new telecommunications regulator is.[11] For the Cartel Office, this has been of no great practical consequence, whereas for the Regulatory Authority for Telecommunications and Posts it has been a critical issue from day one. As the majority shareholder in the traditionally dominant company Deutsche Telekom AG, the state has multi-billion ownership interests. Some quarters claim to detect political pressure in some regulatory rulings to take account of government interest in a successful share sale. The risk of the telecommunications sector—a relatively well-defined sector and, moreover, one which is key to a modern economy—becoming an instrument of industrial policy is relatively great. And the susceptibility of influence by populistically motivated politics is considerable. We need only recall that the German parliament was once called out of recess for a debate on increases in telephone charges.

The constitution does not rule out an independent regulator. The case law of the German Federal Constitutional Court permits so-called minister-free areas, even if to a limited extent only.[12] The crucial aspect would seem to me to be that the independent authority is constrained to pursuing one set of aims stipulated by the law. This is one-dimensional.[13] The legitimacy of such independence would be placed in doubt if the authority were called upon to make discretionary decisions on contentious issues. There is no reliable benchmark for this; it remains a political task, that is to say it falls to an office that, ultimately, is subject to political responsibility via the medium of instructions. In essence, the tasks cited in the TKG are competition-oriented. The overarching task now is to introduce a sector which, for generations, had no contact with competition, into an environment in which competition functions as effectively as possible. Reservations put forward in this and other connections, namely with regard to independent central banks,[14] have to do with democratic theory and show a touch of fundamentalism; they lack conviction. Independent institutions along the lines of the Bundesbank (Federal Bank), of the courts of auditors, of independent agencies such as the Federal Cartel Office and possibly the Regulatory Authority for Telecommunications and Posts, have a stabilising effect within a democratic society. Politics protects itself from itself, as it were. This idea is closely related to the principle of the separation of powers. Viewed thus, independent agencies in the US, for instance, are a frequently encountered, familiar phenomenon.[15]

The TKG itself has opted for an independent regulator. Simply the fact that it is based throughout on the GWB is an indication of this. There, the independence of the Cartel Office may be assumed. Let us just recall one of the many arguments. Despite his powers of authorisation the Minister, in merger control procedures, is bound under established practice by the actual determinations and the assessment of the impact on competition that the Cartel Office makes. He is constrained by the need to address aspects relating to the common good. Such a division of labour would make no sense at all if the Minister could simply order the authority beforehand to clear an intended merger.[16] The genesis of the TKG provides many clues. The final Committee report states the following, for instance: "It is necessary, with regard to the status and independence of the Regulatory Authority, that not every decision can be quashed by the federal ministry to which the Regulatory Authority will be answerable. The independent Ruling Chambers have been introduced for this very reason."[17] In its summing up, a public hearing on the Telecommunications Act speaks of the oft-repeated "importance of the independence of the authority."[18] Reference is made to the "quasi-judicial structure" of proceedings.[19] European Union law demands, moreover, the independence of the national regulatory authority, as long as the "dominant telecommunications organisation" is decisively controlled by the government.[20] An identical requirement is found in No. 5 of the Commitments of the European Communities and their Member States pertaining to the 4th Protocol of 15 April 1997 to the General Agreement on Trade in Services at WTO level (liberalisation of basic telecommunications services). The relevant German law, which required the consent of the *Bundesrat* (upper house of parliament), entered into force on 27 November 1997.[21] As Deutsche Telekom AG is not, at the present moment or for the immediate future, an undertaking that is independent of the state within the meaning of the European regulations cited that are anchored in constitutional and international law, the German TKG legislators are only compliant for as long as provision is made for an independent regulator.[22] The ownership influence of the state will disappear at the latest after the complete privatisation of Deutsche Telekom AG. *Then*, Community law and WTO rules will no longer absolutely demand a regulator that is free of all government influence. Yet that was not the situation facing those drafting the TKG back in 1996. A point of view construing harmony between the legal system and a compliant legislator is not affected by this. In short, then: freedom from ministerial instructions for the Regulatory Authority in its individual rulings is fully justified in my view.

V. EUROPEAN REGULATOR

Finally, the special importance of Community law in the telecommunications sector poses the question whether the necessary regulation would not best be provided by a body operating at Community level, whereby the legislative functions would be separate from the administrative functions.

Two sets of norms must be kept distinct under prevailing law. On the one hand Article 86 of the EC Treaty, and on the other, the approximation of laws as provided for by Article 94 and 95 of the EC Treaty.[23] In Article 86(3) of the EC Treaty, primary Community law empowers the Commission to issue Directives, hence to set its own legislation. It began with the Terminal Directive. Then came the Services Directive. The latter was then amended by three further Directives paving the way for the introduction of full competition in the telecommnications markets on 1 January 1998. Originally, the Member States opposed such extensive legislative powers for the Commission, and contested both the Terminal and the Services Directive before the European Court of Justice, even if unsuccessfully in the main. In this connection, the Commission has limited administrative powers to address individual decisions to Member States in accordance with Article 86(3), and to watch over the application of competition rules, specifically those of Article 82 of the EC Treaty, vis-á-vis the undertakings. As successful as the Commission was and is in the field of telecommunications, it is clear that Article 86 of the EC Treaty will become obsolete in the telecommunications marketplace in the long run. Its applicability presupposes public undertakings or such that have been granted special or exclusive rights. Article 86(2) refers to undertakings entrusted with the operation of services of general economic interest. If, for instance, in Germany the state relinquishes its holding in Deutsche Telekom AG and if the infrastructure requirement of Article 87 f) of the Basic Law (adequate and appropriate telecommunications services throughout the federal territory) is met by market forces, Article 86 will no longer be needed. A European regulator could not be created on this basis.[24]

The legislative organ in the case of approximation according to Article 95 of the EC Treaty is the Council, in other words the sum of the governments of the Member States, not the Commission. The Commission does not have any administrative powers here, either. In telecommunications, Article 95 of the EC Treaty has been invoked for the issue of the many ONP Directives. These have been transposed in

Germany within the framework of the TKG. Here, the EU is not following a strategy of competing regulatory regimes, the principle, as it were, of the country of regulatory origin. This is in accord with the findings that can be derived from the theory of fiscal federalism. Regulation at higher level, a legislative cartel solution, is recommended whenever serious external effects would otherwise occur. Without suitable harmonisation it might be possible for a Member State to benefit from deregulation in another Member State—from the former's point of view a positive external effect which would then reduce the incentive to deregulate—but to make entry to its own country more difficult and thus burden other Member States with the resultant disadvantages—a negative external effect. Agreed, the Community must be prevented from taking the ONP Directives too far. Originally, ONP was devised to facilitate well-functioning competition at the services level, particularly when individual providers held a monopoly position or a dominant position in part of the telecommunications market, when their services and facilities constituted the intermediate input, as it were, for competing providers. Today, the ONP Directives address detailed matters of service quality and seek to push through unified offers such as ISDN throughout the marketplace. An uneasy relationship ensues, such as we are familiar with from standardisation. On the one hand harmonisation makes the market considerably larger, perhaps it is only because of harmonisation that there is a market at all, while on the other there is the typical risk of the emergence of a cartel, meaning that a particular technological solution will be written in stone, stifling the development of other—possibly better—options. In the inevitable balancing act that follows, attention should be drawn away from seeking to answer the question "Is this worthy of being promoted or not?" In the interest of competition it would be preferable to aim to enhance the competitive environment, for example through the extensive unbundling of telecommunications services and facilities.[25]

At the administrative level there is no reason to centralise still further regulation of the European telecommunications market. Decentralised administration provides better information. The task at European level, specifically for the Commission, will be to supervise the national regulatory authorities in respect of the proper application of uniform rules. At best, centralisation is conceivable in the case of original providers of Europe-wide or international services. This is the rationale underlying one-stop-shopping. I am thinking here, for instance, of communication via low earth orbit satellites, of the Iridium, Globalstar, ICO and Teledesic projects, for example.

When the Regulatory Authority for Telecommunications and Posts was first introduced to the public on 7 January 1998 the then Economics Minister expressed the view that the new authority should "gradually make itself redundant."[26] This intent is reflected in the TKG by the requirement on the Monopolies Commission to investigate whether there is workable competition in the telecommunications markets and whether it will entail consequences for individual provisions of the TKG, most notably whether the rulings on rates regulation continue to be necessary (Section 81(3) of the TKG). The wording "for individual provisions" denotes a realistic perspective: The TKG as a whole will not become obsolete so quickly. Yet it is entirely possible that, as competition increases, particularly at long-distance level, the Regulatory Authority's powers will need to be reduced accordingly.

ENDNOTES

[1] *Biedenkopf,* Staatliche Selbstbeschränkung als Prinzip einer zukunftsoffenen Kommunikationsordnung, Manuscript for a speech delivered to the International Symposium of the Bertelsmann Foundation on 9/10 September 1998 in Gütersloh; see also FAZ No. 210 of 10 September 1998, p. 19.

[2] CDU/CSU, SPD and F.D.P., Draft Telecommunications Act (TKG), Bundestag Printed Paper 13/3609 (1996), pertaining to Section 2 = p. 36, lower right-hand column.

[3] Likewise the *Monopolies Commission,* 12th Report, 1998, point 22; *Möschel,* Zwischen Konflikt und Kooperation: Regulierungszuständigkeiten in der Telekommunikation, in: Multimedia: Kommunikation ohne Grenzen – grenzenloser Wettbewerb?, published by FIW, 1998, p. 53, 54; *Schuster* in BeckTKG-Kommentar, 1997, Section 2 sidenote 32; for a different opinion see: *Geppert,* in: BeckTKG-Kommentar, 1997, Section 82 side-

note 15; *Gramlich,* Entwicklungen der staatlichen Wirtschaftsaufsicht: das Telekommunikationsrecht als Modell, Verwaltungsarchiv 1997, 598, 641.

[4] Cf. *Monopolies Commission,* 12th Report, 1998, point 23, 519 et s.

[5] *Mestmäcker/Witte*, Gutachten zur Zuständigkeit für die Verhaltensaufsicht nach dem dritten und vierten Teil des Referentenentwurfs für ein Telekommunikationsgesetz vom 22.11.1995, typescript, p. 11 (4th paragraph) and p. 42 (1st paragraph).

[6] This was also clear to those drafting the TKG, cf. section-by-section analysis (footnote 2), p. 37 upper left-hand column, 2nd paragraph.

7 A view put forward by the Competition Commissioner Karel Van Miert, Probleme der wettbewerblichen Öffnung von Märkten mit Netzstrukturen aus europäischer Sicht, WuW 1998, 7, 12; see too Commission notice on the application of the competition rules to access agreements in the telecommunications sector - Framework, relevant markets and principles, OJ 1998 C 265/2 et s., here p. 4 et s. The Commission's low profile is a result of the idea - in keeping with the principle of subsidiarity (Article 3 b(1) of the EC Treaty) - of extending the decentralised application of European competition law, cf. Commission notice on cooperation between the national competition authorities and the Commission in handling cases falling within the scope of Articles 85 or 86 of the EC Treaty, OJ 1997 313/3-11.

[8] *Möschel* (Footnote 3), p. 58. On the criteria for rates regulation in accordance with Section 24 of the TKG see also *Schuster/Stürmer,* in: BeckTKG-Komm. (Footnote 3), Section 24 sidenote 24.

[9] ECJ 4.5.1988, ECR 1988, 2479, 2515 et s. Bodson; 23.4.1991, ECR 1991 I-1979, 2015 et s. Arbeitsvermittlungsmonopol; cf. *Möschel,* Hoheitliche Maßnahmen und die Wettbewerbsvorschriften des Gemeinschaftsrechts, in Weiterentwicklung der Europäischen Gemeinschaften und der Marktwirtschaft, published by FIW 1992, p. 89, p. 95 et s.; *idem* in Immenga/Mestmäcker EG-Wettbewerbsrecht, Kommentar Vol. I, 1997, Art. 86 sidenote 10; for more details see *Mestmäcker*, ibid, Vol. II, Art. 90(1) sidenotes 51, 55 and 68 with extensive documentation; see too *idem*, Kommunikation ohne Monopole II, 1995, p. 13, 123 et s.

[10] Cf. Art. 2 of the Commission's Transparency Directive 80/723/EEC, OJ 1980 L 195/35, last amended by Directive 93/84/EEC, OJ 1993 L 254/16. The ECJ has approved the definition contained therein, related to the purposes of the Directive, cf. 6.7.1982, Case 188-190/80, ECR 1982, 2545, 2579 - Transparency Directive; in the literature, however, it is considered capable of generalisation, cf. *Mestmäcker*, Staat und Unternehmen im Gemeinschaftsrecht. On the importance of Art. 90 of the EC Treaty see RabelsZ 52 (1988), 526, 556.

[11] On the subject of independence see *Müller-Terpitz*, Die Regulierungsbehörde für den Telekommunikationsmarkt, Summary 1997, 257, 272; *Lerche*, in Maunz/Dürig/Herzog (editors), Grundgesetz Kommentar, October 1996, Art. 87 et s. Sidenote 112; *Schrader*, Der neue ordnungspolitische Rahmen für die Telekommunikationsmärkte, in Witte (editor), Das Telekommunikationsgesetz 1996. Eine Herausforderung für Markt und Ordnungspolitik, 1996, p. 35, 41 et s.; for a different opinion see: *Gramlich,* Ohne Regulierung kein Wettbewerb, Zum Start der Regulierungsbehörde für Telekommunikation und Post, CR 1998, 463, 464 et s.; *Moritz/Neus*, Telekommunikationsgesetz und US-Telecommunications Act: Ein Vergleich der ordnungspolitischen Ansätze, CR 1997, 239, 244; *Nolte*, Lizenzierung von Telekommunikationsunternehmen, CR 1996, 459, 464.

[12] BVerfGE 9, 268, 281 et s.; 22, 106, 113 et s.; 83, 130, 149 et s.

[13] For more on this aspect see *Möschel*, Die Unabhängigkeit des Bundeskartellamtes, ORDO 48 (1997), 241, 244 et s.; *idem,* (Footnote 3), p. 60. Likewise Federal Bank President *Tietmeyer,* cf. FAZ No. 258 of 6 November 1998, p. 1.

[14] Cf. for instance *Barbier*, Münzen und Monstranzen: Kampf um die Idee Bundesbank: Eine Art Religionskrieg, FAZ No. 19 of 23 Jan. 1997, p. 23.

[15] Cf. *Möschel,* (Footnote 13), p. 248 et s.

[16] For a more detailed account of the whole see *Möschel,* (Footnote 13), p. 241 et s.

[17] Recommended decision and report by the Committee on Posts and Telecommunications, Bundestag printed paper 13/4864, p. 82; also the then Federal Economics Minister *Günter Rexrodt*, speech delivered on 7.1.1998 on the occasion of the introduction of the Regulatory Authority for Telecommunications and Posts to the public, printed in Zentralverband Elektrotechnik und Elektroindustrie e.V., Circular letter FJ 8/98, Annex 1, and the President of the new Regulatory Authority, *Klaus-Dieter Scheuerle*, Regulierungsbehörde für Telekommunikation und Post nimmt Arbeit auf, MMR 1998, VII, hold the view that the Regulatory Authority is independent.

[18] Loco citato (Footnote 17), p. 72.

[19] Section-by-section analysis of the Act (Footnote 2), p. 51.

[20] Cf. Art. 7(1) of the Services Directive 90/388/EEC, OJ 1990 L 192/10; Communication by the Commission to the European Parliament and the Council on the status and implementation of Directive 90/388/EEC on competition in the markets for telecommunications services, OJ 1995 C 275/2, 10; likewise Art. 2(2) of Council Directive on the application of open network provision (ONP) to voice telephony (95/62/EEC), OJ 1995 L 321/6; see also Commission notice (Footnote 7), p. 4.

[21] Federal Law Gazette 1997 II, 1990 et s.

[22] For a different opinion see: *Gramlich* (Footnote 11), p. 464 et s.: legal independence is not required.

[23] Cf. *Van Miert* (Footnote 7), p. 8 et s.

[24] Cf. *Möschel* (Footnote 3), p. 62.

[25] Cf. *Knorr*, Sieben Thesen zur Standardisierungspolitik in der Telekommunikation, in Mestmäcker, Kommunikation ohne Monopole II, 1995, p. 515, 523 et s.

[26] *Rexrodt* (Footnote 7).

2

THE PATH TO COMPETITION FOR TELECOMMUNICATIONS IN GERMANY

Christoph Engel
Max-Planck-Project Group
University of Osnabrück

Will telecommunications in Germany remain imprisoned by its own history? Did the legislature open the prison door in vain when it lifted the telecommunications monopoly? Have the decades of imprisonment rendered it too weak to stand on its own two feet? This is how telecommunications in Germany is portrayed by many[1], including its regulatory authority[2]. The legislature rightfully exercises more care. Instead of imposing the transition to competition from above; it restricts itself to a tailor-made correction of the specific competitive problems of the transition (I). This particularly applies to the heavily-disputed case surrounding the right of a new provider to unbundled access to the local loop belonging to Telekom (II).

I. BASIC DECISIONS

The regulatory objectives are specifically defined by the Basic Law (*Grundgesetz*) and the Telecommunications Act (*Telekommunikationsgesetz, or TKG*) (1). For this purpose, they count not only on competition between services but also between physical networks (2). The Telecommunications Act dispenses with asymmetric regulation at the expense of Telekom (3). Instead, it finds solutions to the specific competitive problems arising from the transition from a legally-protected monopoly to a competitive enterprise (4). The legislature was less fortunate when it opted for sector-specific regulation (5). And it was not sufficiently conscious of the inherent limitations of government interventions (6).

1. Regulatory Objectives

According to prevailing opinion, and in contrast with European Community law,[3] there is no compulsion on the German legislature to state exactly what objectives it pursues. Nevertheless, modern laws do precisely this more and more frequently.[4] The Telecommunications Act follows this tradition. Its first paragraph reads:

> The purpose of this law is to promote competition in the telecommunications sector via regulation and ensure the provision of suitable and adequate services on a nation-wide basis, as well as to allocate frequencies.

The law thereby clarifies the somewhat murky formulations of Art. 87 f of the Basic Law. Frequency allocation plays no role for this paper[5]. The other provisions of the law serve two objectives: market creation and market correction. The first, competition objective has its constitutional roots in Art. 87 f II Basic Law[6]; the second, public welfare objective in Art. 87 f I Basic Law. The precise interpretation of this latter objective plays no role here[7]; it is sufficient to recognize that the legislature pursues these two objectives with separate instruments. The provisions of §§ 17 – 22 TKG concerning universal services serve the public welfare objective, whereas the regulations of §§ 23 – 39

TKG exclusively serve the competition objective. Open network access and monetary regulation are thus reactions of the legislature to competition problems, and must not be masked by public welfare objectives.[8]

The Telecommunications Act goes even further. It also makes a decision in favor of a certain model of competition policy[9]. This is most apparent in a somewhat concealed place, namely, § 81 III 1 TKG, in which the monopolies commission is directed to examine the question every two years, "whether workable competition exists in the telecommunications markets." The law therefore specifically does not pursue the utopia of perfect competition. Its objective is not a market structure that is broken down into atomic particles. It is instead sufficient to have just a few providers, of perhaps unequal strength, as long as none of them can maneuver their behavior in a manner that is no longer adequately controlled by the competition. At the same time, it follows from this that the law does not necessarily seek to alter the current market structure. Potential or substitutive competition can suffice. The law considers the threat of entry by potential competitors to be as serious as the competitive pressure from neighboring markets. The law is also not static in regard to another aspect: it does not merely observe the communications markets that have been handed-down to it. On the contrary, it places its stakes on the welfare gains to be expected if the geographic or substantive boundaries of the market become permeable. It therefore expressly desires competition that is oriented towards market creation and innovation. It can make equal use of the convergence between different telecommunications services and the globalization of telecommunications markets. That the legislature counts on these dynamics, is again apparent in the previously cited provision § 81 III 1 TKG.

2. Service and Infrastructure Competition

Service and infrastructure competition are often contrasted with one another in the political discussion surrounding telecommunications[10]. This is slanted. Of course the Telecommunications Act continues to aim for competition between services. Anyone wishing to bring valued-added services via the networks of Deutsche Telekom or its competitors is just as welcome as a reseller, who sells telecommunications services from the established suppliers on his own account. Competition among services was therefore not merely a historic transition period from older telecommunications reforms that did not at that stage aim to touch the network monopoly.

But the difference between the Telecommunications Act and previous statutes is that it is not exclusively aimed at competition between services. It differentiates itself from these laws precisely in that infrastructure competition is now also possible. This is visible of course by the express abolition of the telecommunications monopoly in § 1 of the old Telecommunications Systems Act (*Fernmeldeanlagengesetz)*. The significance of the Telecommunications Act is, however, not restricted to just this one aspect. If the legislature had gone on the assumption that network competition is totally impractical, it would have had to link up the abolition of the telecommunications monopoly with a regulatory instrument known from other similarly-structured branches. In these branches, instead of competing within the market, the players compete for the market. The state awards a monopoly to a provider for a fixed timeframe, which is periodically awarded in a tender competition. German law has primarily gathered experience with this instrument in the radio sector. This is how terrestrial radio frequencies are allotted within the terms of the state media laws[11]. The Telecommunications Act proceeds in a different manner, as is particularly apparent in §§ 36 and 37. According to these provisions, all operators of public telecommunications networks are obliged to enter negotiations with each another regarding the connection of their networks. If these negotiations do not meet their objective, the connection can be dictated by the regulatory authority.

The statute's decision in favor of both service and network competition is not only dogmatically clear; it also makes economic sense, since it is only the competition between networks that is sustainable. Only competition between networks can forego elaborate governance structures for the relationship between network operators and service providers. Only network competition, therefore, makes regulation superfluous in the long term[12] .

3. *Forgoing Asymmetric Regulation*

Court proceedings are where statutes unfold and evolve. This is where the legal system gathers the experience that it needs in order to make the statute operational. For this, however, the legal system pays a price, since it is the unhealthy cases that come before it, not the healthy ones. The conflict between the parties must have reached such a level as to place a compromise out of reach. The genuine social function of the courts is to end this conflict, in which a central role is played by the result that each party can be expected to bear. If he cannot bring the parties to agree on a settlement, the judge must find this result within the terms of the existing laws. This interpretation then affects the much more common cases, in which peace under the law is not at all in jeopardy. The application by the courts therefore systematically tilts the law in the direction of equity considerations. This is one of the most important arguments for integrating law and institutional economics, since with the aid of institutional economics, a lawyer has a chance to forecast the effects of a proposed construction in standard situations.

All the above has a bearing on our question. In the disputes between Telekom and its competitors, it is repeatedly argued that Telekom's network has already been paid for in the past by its customers. Telekom can therefore be expected to subject itself to state intervention.

Even the starting point is partly wrong. When privatization took place, considerable portions of its investments in the network had not yet been amortized: one only has to think of the glass fiber network in the new *Länder*. But the law is—rightly—primarily concerned with workable competition, and not with the burdens to be borne by each party. It looks at the future and not the past. This is particularly appropriate insofar as Telekom shares have already been sold on the stock exchange. The general public has, so to speak, already made a profit and reaped the benefit in current terms of past investments.

If one looks at the future, asymmetric regulation is nothing more than industrial policy. The firms involved are specifically treated unequally, with the supposedly weaker ones enjoying more favorable treatment in the form of legal protection zones against competition. Put differently: the state artificially lowers the entry barriers to the market. The market entry costs of the competitors are precisely lowered by the obligation of the incumbent to provide them assistance.

As a consequence, asymmetric regulation shares all the disadvantages that otherwise adhere to industrial policies of the state.[13] Of particular importance is the knowledge problem. How can the state recognize whether a competitor really needs assistance or whether it just puts forward an argument in order to score an advantage over Telekom? Moreover, positive discrimination provides an incentive to new competitors to turn regulation into a permanent state of affairs.

There is no alteration to the judgment if one interprets asymmetric regulation, in the context of competition policy terminology, as a means of creating a counterweight. This concept is also nowhere to be found in the statute. Such an active competition policy would be problematic for the same reasons as industrial policy. There is no reason why the regulator should possess superior knowledge about developments in the market. The legal system would again provide an impulse to make regulation a permanent state. What is more, a neighboring economy has had a bad experience with this concept. In England, British Telecom's telecommunications monopoly was initially only lifted on a partial basis. Only one competitor for domestic and another for foreign traffic, namely Mercury and Sprint respectively, were allowed to compete with it side-by-side. At the outset, thanks to legal protection barriers, these firms enjoyed a market share of around 5% yet, against the regulators' expectations, they also stuck at more or less the same market share in the long term[14]. The new competitors have carved themselves out a niche. Oligopoly theory, which is based on game theory, can explain why this result is far from astonishing[15].

4. *Solutions to Competition Problems in the Transition from a Legally Protected Monopoly*

Declining asymmetric regulation does not, however, mean that the legal system can limit itself to lifting the monopoly's legal protection. The transition from a legally-protected monopoly to competition creates specific competition problems. The task of competition law is to identify these problems and find customized solutions to them. In the language of *Günter Knieps*: competition policy should follow a disaggregate approach[16]. We must ensure, however, that we do not artificially restrict our view. The after-effects of the legal barrier to market entry (see (a) p. 21) can either be increased via simultaneous structural barriers to market entry (see (b) p. 24) or weakened by the peculiarities of the markets (see (c) p. 24).

a) After-effects of the legal barrier to market entry

At the moment the telecommunications monopoly was abandoned, there was only one supplier in each of the newly-opened telecommunications markets: Deutsche Telekom. In this situation, competitive pressure was mainly exerted by potential competition[17]. Its intensity depended on what economic market entry barriers still existed after the lifting of the legal barrier to market entry.

The attention of the legal system is primarily attracted by Deutsche Telekom's high market share, which initially necessarily amounts to 100%. But precisely this is nothing extraordinary during the transition from a monopoly to a competitive enterprise. Moreover, monopolies can also be created under competition. In local and regional markets they are in practice even relatively common. One only has to consider municipalities with just one newspaper. German law treats a monopoly as a particular case of a dominant position. In §§ 19 and 20 Antitrust Act (*Gesetz gegen Wettbewerbsbeschränkungen - GWB*)[18] it subordinates market dominant suppliers to a check against abuse. German law specifically avoids intervention in a market's structure, and does not recognize the concept of demonopolization. German law has consciously made no exception to this during telecommunications deregulation and privatization. One may express regret in this case, but the interpreter of the law is bound by it.

The legislature has even gone a step further in privatizing Telekom as a vertically-integrated company. Telekom may therefore continue to offer network services and equipment from a single source. The legislature has apparently placed a high value on the advantages of bundling. A specific competition problem then indeed arises. § 33 TKG is the customized solution to this problem. This provision forms the subject of the second part of this analysis[19].

When a new competitor restricts itself to offering telecommunications services, it is forced to accept Telekom's existing network as it stands. The same thing applies to a new network operator, who cannot initially cover the whole area. These competitors have repeatedly asserted that the technical parameters of Telekom's network do not correspond to their business concepts; innovative services cannot be offered on the old network. This assertion does not always apply, but will do so increasingly. This is, however, the main incentive for competing networks. Precisely if this is the only possibility for offering a profitable new service, it becomes rational to build a new network. Formulated another way: competitors' business concepts cannot and should not determine the future technical design of Deutsche Telekom's network.

However, a further misgiving of the new competitors is serious. In the process of switching, the incumbent network operator gains data on the connections made, from which it can theoretically draw conclusions about its competitors' strategies. In the extreme, it would even be able to determine with which subscribers they have done business and react to this knowledge with a counter-offer. In terms of competition policy, this is an instance of market intransparency being a prerequisite for workable competition. Technical safeguards are called for in this case[20] to ensure secrecy. No specific regulations on this aspect have been incorporated into the Telecommunications Act. One must therefore revert to the general provisions of the Antitrust Act on the abuse of dominant positions. It would be an abuse of power if Telekom, as a competitor in the markets for telecommunications networks and services, exploited this information. According to § 32, in conjunction with § 19 I GWB, the Federal Cartel Office (*Bundeskartellamt*) could intervene against this behavior.

That someone submits a better or cheaper offer than the established provider, does not necessarily mean that it will automatically attract customers away from the latter. This is due to the fact that there are often costs associated with a change of supplier. The subscriber has also gained experience with his present supplier, whereas the reliability of a new supplier is necessarily uncertain. Customers' laziness is therefore often attributable to quite rational reasons. In addition, end-users are not subject to competitive pressures and can afford not to react immediately to price cuts. The legislature has taken note of the most important expression of this problem. According to § 43 V TKG, anyone changing his provider may retain his telephone number. He is therefore not forced to notify all his friends and business contacts that he has a new number[21].

Finally, the economic value of a telecommunications network is not merely related to the possibility of transporting signals between two points. Moreover, a network becomes more valuable the greater the number of persons using it. A dynamic problem leads on from these network externalities—the problem of critical mass. Anyone setting up a new telecommunications network must therefore conduct a type of expectations management. The first customers do not profit from the network much at this point. For every potential customer it is therefore rational to wait and see whether the new service succeeds. Since this is the case, a provider must make credible commitments that it is not going to give up prematurely, thereby causing its first customers to have incurred only costs and scarcely profited from its use. This problem has also attracted the attention of the law. In accordance with § 35 TKG, bidders have a right to demand that calls originating in their own network be handed over to the incumbent's networks and vice versa. In this manner, the network effects are, so to speak, socialized[22].

b) Strengthening via structural barriers to market entry

A company that is pondering whether or not to become a new entrant in a telecommunications market will not only, and not even primarily, glance at the peculiarities listed above in the transition from a legally-protected monopoly. Much more important factors are the economies of scale and the sunk costs associated with market entry. Both are particularly significant for the operation of telecommunications networks. Because of the network externalities already mentioned above, a small network has, as a rule, only little value for its users. And the majority of costs for the provision of network services are fixed. The provider must thus absorb costs in one go at the commencement of business activity. This is so significant, because telecommunications networks can hardly be used for other purposes.

c) Weakening via idiosyncrasies of telecommunications markets

In other structurally-related markets, these idiosyncrasies have made potential competition very weak. Railways are a good example. Telecommunications markets, however, are different due to their highly dynamic character. The dynamism roots in rapid technological and economic progress. In addition, until now, the telecommunications monopoly had prevented competition from neighboring markets. Since it was lifted, it has been seen that this competition is very intense. It comes in the form of substitution competition from alternative nets. As is known, it is primarily electricity providers and also the *Deutsche*

Bahn (German Railways) that have decided to enter the market, because they themselves already possess developed telecommunications networks. Substitution competition receives added impulses from the convergence between differing telecommunications services and between telecommunications services and the content that is transported via them. One example is the merging of individual and mass communication via the Internet.

More competitive pressure originates from both neighboring product and geographic markets. Since Deutsche Telekom has already covered the whole country, we are in practical terms concerned at this juncture with competition from abroad. Former foreign monopolists are partly pushing into the German market themselves and they are partly seeking co-operative ventures with new German providers.

Finally, the new communications providers profit from the blessing of a late birth. They enter the competition, economically speaking, without having incurred stranded costs. They can thus build communications networks in accordance with today's technical and economic requirements. They have no old investments whose costs must first be recovered, and they are also not burdened by an excess of personnel by today's standards.

5. *General or Sector-specific Regulation?*

The Telecommunications Act has not only created specific rules and a regulatory authority for the needs of the general public, but also for the competition problems of the branch (a). A practicing lawyer cannot ignore them, but he can interpret them as narrowly as possible (b).

a) The text of the statute

Article One of the Telecommunications Act, as we already know, permits no doubt as to the double intention of the law. It not only serves the demands of the general public, but also those of competition policy. The legislature has thus created sector-specific antitrust rules.

Going even further, the legislature has left the application of these sector-specific rules to the regulatory authority for telecommunications and postal services (*Regulierungsbehörde für das Post- und Telekommunikationswesen*) and not the Federal Cartel Office.

Nonetheless, the legislature has not hermetically sealed off the sector-specific rules from those of general antitrust law. On the contrary, a type of double-barrier doctrine results from § 2 III TKG: the competitive behavior of telecommunications providers must satisfy the sector-specific provisions of the TKG and also the general provisions of the GWB. § 82 TKG goes even further than this. It obliges the regulatory authority and the cartel office to harmonize their positions in interpreting substantive law and to co-operate in antitrust proceedings. Last, but not least, § 81 III TKG makes the provisional character of the sector-specific rules apparent. The monopolies commission is required to make a statement every two years on whether regulation of this specific sector continues to be necessary.

b) Restrictive interpretation

Even when one takes this cushioning into consideration, the decision in favor of the Telecommunications Act is an unfortunate one. Even as it stood at the time when the Telecommunications Act was passed, the Antitrust Act would mostly have been adequate to overcome the specific problems arising from the transition to competition. Even under the GWB, the aim is not one of perfect competition. When the question of the underlying model of competition comes up, jurisprudence decides in favor of workable competition[23]. Long-standing dominant positions are no peculiarity of the telecommunications market.

With the sixth amendment that has just been passed, both statutes come even closer to each other, in that the so-called Essential Facilities Doctrine has now been incorporated into § 19 IV No. 4 GWB as well. General antitrust law thus also contains an instrument for the specific competition problems arising from the vertical integration of a company that is dominant in the market. The remaining instruments that have already been mentioned, such as the portability of numbers and the compulsory connection of networks, could equally have been absorbed into the GWB.

This would have been preferable because sector-specific antitrust law is burdened with considerable disadvantages. It invites companies to pursue a game of tactics with different statutes and authorities. Double costs for the application of the law arise for both companies and the state. A great danger exists that, ultimately, the competition policy objective and the general welfare objective of the Telecommunications Act will become blurred. There is also the worry that the regulatory authority will have no easy access to the knowledge and experience gained by the Federal Cartel Office with similar market constellations in other branches. If the Cartel Office was responsible for the application of the antitrust provisions in the Telecommunications Act, the results would have to be measured daily against the solutions achieved for other branches, taken by the neighboring chambers of the same authority. In hiving off telecommunications oversight to a separate regulatory authority, the danger exists that the regulators' angle of vision will narrow. Nor can the regulatory authority avail itself of the services of the other decision chambers as a type of self-control mechanism. Social psychology can put this more precisely: telecommunications' regulators do not belong to the same peer group as the regulators of other branches.

Finally, its hiving off leads to a change in the relationship between the authority and the companies. The opportunity for the companies to pull the authority, so to speak, into the boat becomes much greater. In the worst case, it comes to what political scientists call 'capture.' The authority is then merely the extended arm of the companies. The situation hardly improves if the authority allows itself to be pushed into a type of entrepreneurial co-responsibility. Finally, the economic theory of bureaucracies points to a further cause for concern. The existence of a regulatory authority depends namely on the existence of regulation pertinent to a specific branch. In well-understood self-interest, it must therefore pay attention to interpreting these norms in such a way as to expand its area of competence and secure its long-term existence. The decisions of the regulatory authority concerning competitors' unbundled access to Telekom's subscriber lines fit into this picture well.

Lawyers therefore have every reason to keep the sector-specific antitrust provisions of the TKG as tightly as possible in line with the body of knowledge accumulated in the GWB. If possible, they should interpret these norms in such a way as to make them superfluous by themselves. The monopolies commission should urge the legislature to incorporate the sector-specific rules as quickly as possible into the GWB and only leave the regulatory authority the task of looking after the public interest.

6. Boundaries of Regulation

Ultimately, the telecommunications regulators should show a greater awareness of the limitations inherent in their activity. For sure, this is a political rather than a legal exhortation, but it provides the reasoning for applying the instruments of the statute in a skeptical, rather than a euphoric fashion.

Regulation is limited by the problems of knowledge and enforcement. The knowledge barriers result, economically speaking, from information asymmetries. At best, the regulator can only come close to roughly approximating costs, opportunity costs, value-creating factors, marketing opportunities and prices. In most cases where this information is lacking, it is difficult to determine the need for regulation. It is even harder to determine what can be deemed an adequate reaction of the legal system. This will be demonstrated in the analysis of the dispute concerning access to local loops.

The enforcement problem arises primarily from the open foreign flank. Under international law, sealing off German sovereign territory may appear permissible[24]. Politically, however, it is unthinkable, and regularly also technically out of the question. So foreign telecommunications companies flood onto the German market and telecommunications traffic is routed via foreign territory or via satellite, if domestic regulation is too strict. Moreover, the telecommunications authority has a type of factual open flank. This results from the convergence of telecommunications with branches that are no longer subject to the jurisdiction of the authority. This has practical significance primarily in the convergence between telecommunications transport and telecommunications contents.

II. CASE STUDY: DISPUTE SURROUNDING UNBUNDLED ACCESS TO LOCAL LOOPS

None of this is just pure theory. A whole range of conflicts is already being fought out between Telekom and its competitors, using telecommunications laws as the means. The dispute concerning unbundled access to local loops has even proceeded as far as the courts. The administrative court in Cologne and the higher administrative court in Münster have basically ruled against Telekom[25]. The case is set out shortly below (1). §33 TKG proves itself to be a customized solution to the competition problem on which this case is based (2), since the regulation incorporates the Essential Facilities Doctrine of American antitrust law into German law (3). The same result is reached if one instead weighs up all the interests in the open (4).

1. Summary of the Case

Only Telekom possesses nation-wide local networks. Nowadays, in some local networks, there are two competing network operators. Up until now, these local networks have not been run by competitors of Telekom that compete with it for long-distance calls. These long-distance competitors, and some of the local-network competitors, have demanded access to Telekom's local networks. They seek "unbundled" access, i.e. only the physical, not the logical connections to the networks. In short, they are seeking the bare wires. They underpin their demands with § 33 TKG. The underlying interpretation of the provision is false[26].

2. § 33 TKG as the Customized Solution

§ 33 paragraph 1, sentence one, TKG reads:

> *Special Supervision Against Abuse.* A provider who possesses a dominant position in a market, as defined by § 22 GWB, for telecommunications services for the general public must permit competitors, without discrimination, access to the facilities it uses internally and offers in the market, as long as they are essential, at those conditions it grants to itself for the use of these services in order to provide other telecommunications services, unless the granting of less favorable conditions, in particular the imposition of restrictions, is objectively justifiable.

The provision is a linguistic monster. If one separates it into its components, it can be seen, however, that it represents a customized solution for the transitional competition problem. The problem results from the fact that Telekom has been unleashed into the competitive field as a vertically-integrated enterprise.

The provision can be split into five elements. It makes statements about the addressee. It is directed against vertically-integrated companies, who are simultaneously active in a competitive market and also in the monopolistic bottleneck one step further back in the value chain. It is further presupposed that the addressee dominates the competitive market. Secondly, the provision identifies the claimant. Every competitor in the competitive market is entitled to sue the dominant provider. Thirdly, the provision identifies the prerequisites for a claim: from an economic point of view, simultaneous access to the complementary market is essential for access to the competitive market. Fourth, if these provisions are satisfied, § 33 TKG determines as the basis for the claim that the dominant provider enters into the market for the intermediate service and must place it at the disposal of its competitors without discrimination. And fifth, the norm contains a justification clause.

The structure of complicated norms can be elucidated much more easily graphically than verbally. The following assessment scheme is therefore appended:

1. Addressee
   vertically-integrated enterprise that is simultaneously active in
   aa) competitive market
   bb) monopolistic bottleneck for intermediate service
   [b) Domination of the competitive market]

2. Claimant
   Competitor in the competitive market

3. Prerequisite for a claim
   Simultaneous access to the complementary market is essential for access to the competitive market

4. Basis of a claim
   Compulsion to enter the market for the intermediate service
   Freedom from discrimination

[5. Justification clause]

3. § 33 TKG as a Case Study of the Essential Facilities Doctrine

If one leaves out the points in square brackets, we obtain a precise picture of the Essential Facilities Doctrine in American antitrust law[27]. This is no accident, since this doctrine precisely seeks to overcome the competition problem with which German telecommunications is also now confronted in the transition from a monopoly to competition.

The doctrine has the following parameters: a monopolistic bottleneck exists and the coupling of both products is necessary for entry into the open market. A monopolistic bottleneck is characterized by the fact that an incontestable natural monopoly exists. Both conditions must be satisfied simultaneously. If only a natural monopoly exists, but it is one that can be contested, the monopolist is sufficiently policed by potential competitors.

A natural monopoly exists when a single supplier can produce more cheaply than several. The relevant part of demand is characterized by economies of scale and scope[28]. The determination of a natural monopoly is therefore an empirical question, more precisely, a prognostic one, since antitrust law seeks to have an effect on the future of the markets. In the end, no regulatory authority in the world can know the outcome. This skepticism has particular significance for telecommunications, because here products and markets move rapidly. But a standard in antitrust law cannot depend on that. The fact that a competition problem could possibly be resolved by itself one day, is of no use to competitors as long as it does not actually occur. Just as in merger control cases, the application of § 33 TKG should be geared to the time-frame prognosis that is relevant for competition policy, i.e. between three and five years.

Whether or not a natural monopoly can be contested, depends on the level of sunk costs. Anyone forced to make a huge initial investment that is lost upon exiting the market will consider very carefully, whether or not to enter the market.

§ 33 TKG is, however, not generally concerned with monopolistic bottlenecks. It is more concerned with the consequences that result when an enterprise simultaneously enjoys a monopolistic bottleneck and is active in a preceding or successive competitive market. The provision seeks to prevent the enterprise from transferring its market power from one market to another.

The above is only possible if the coupling of both products is necessary for entry into the open market. Whether this is so, depends on the demand structure. If the customers for the competitive product are namely prepared to purchase it on its own, the monopolistic bottleneck will have no effect on this market. It is a different case if customers insist on obtaining both products from one supplier. In the telecommunications area, one speaks of one-stop shopping and also of one-stop billing. In actual fact, that is probably often the case, since customers save themselves transaction costs in this manner. They have only one contract partner and do not need to worry whether the different components are compatible with each other. Above all, they protect themselves from the strategic behavior of the owner of the bottleneck resource. The components sold in the competitive market are namely only of use to customers if they also simultaneously receive access to the bottleneck resource. They would therefore be subject to blackmail by an isolated provider of such a resource.

If the conditions of the Essential Facilities Doctrine exist, § 33 TKG grants the competitors in the competitive market the right to demand supplies of the bottleneck resource from the vertically-integrated enterprise. That is a considerable intervention in the latter's competitive freedom since, on its own, the vertically-integrated enterprise would not offer the bottleneck component as an intermediate service to other businesses. § 33 TKG thus forces the vertically-integrated company to open the market for the intermediate service.

§ 33 TKG states precisely at what prices and conditions this is to take place: "free of discrimination." Competitors must therefore purchase the intermediate service as it is. The regulatory authority has no competence to set tariff regulations and could not, for example, introduce price-capping. Moreover, the price is derived from the true production costs of the vertically-integrated enterprise.

But where does the border lie between the monopolistic bottleneck and the competitive market? How far should the product offered by the vertically-integrated business be unbundled? The following three sketches assist in arriving at an answer:

Value-creation stages

		Local call	Long-distance call
Transport	At the source location	+	+
	At the destination location		+
	Long-distance		+
Switching		+	+
Accessibility	Active	+	+
	Passive	+	+
		Local call	Long-distance call

Pre-selection and call-by-call (§ 43 VI TKG)

		Local call	Long-distance call
Transport	At the source location	Telekom	Telekom
	At the destination location	–	Telekom
	Long-distance	–	Competitor
Switching		Telekom	Both
Accessibility	Active	Telekom	Both
	Passive	Telekom	Both
		Local call	Long-distance call

Unbundled access (§ 33 I TKG)

		Local call	Long-distance call
Transport	At the source location	Telekom	<Telekom>
	At the destination location	–	<Telekom>
	Long-distance	–	Competitor
Switching		Telekom	Both
Accessibility	Active	Telekom	Both
	Passive	Telekom	Both

<Telekom>: Difference between its technical form and its form under private law: Telekom acts as a performance aid.

We can make the following deductions from the above diagrams: Right from the outset, local calls are of no concern whatsoever. A competitor only provides long-distance transport for the long-distance phone calls it makes on its own behalf. It is always Telekom's task to transport these calls locally at both the source and destination locations. Telekom and its competitors both contribute to the switching services and their availability. As long as end users demand a bundled product, customers are not made aware of this technical and economic state. Their contract partner for long-distance calls is exclusively Telekom's long-distance network competitor. Legally speaking, Telekom is the competitor's performance aid.

And thus the answer to the degree of unbundling becomes apparent. By itself, a competitor can only offer the long-distance transport and pertinent switching capabilities, as well as the accessibility that is produced by this. Were this not the case, the prerequisites for a claim would already be missing. From this we conclude: a competitor can only demand access to the local networks as a whole, i.e. including Telekom's local switching capabilities. In this, it must accept Telekom's network in the condition in which it finds it. It can neither use a network of another quality nor one that has been manufactured more economically. Everything else would no longer represent a non-discriminatory service—it would instead represent the subsidization of competitors via Telekom's services. The law does not extend that far.

4. Trade-off Analysis

We have now reached the end of our analysis from the simultaneous viewpoints of legal dogmatism and competition policy. But it is well-known that lawyers are careful individuals. In case they have not convinced someone with the main thread of their argument, they like to put forward a second line: in our case, a definitional element of § 33 TKG, of which we have so far had no need. The provision ends namely with a justification clause. The right to access the network is granted to competitors "unless [worse treatment] is objectively justified." With this formulation, the Telecommunications Act leans closely on the discrimination prohibition of general antitrust law. It is included in § 20 I GWB[29]. In antitrust law, the necessity of a comprehensive weighing up of interests can be derived from this characteristic[30].

In the legal discussion, the weighing up of interests under antitrust law is often reduced to the weighing up of reasonable burdens. That is a backward-looking interpretation inspired by distribution politics. It is just as unfitting here as it is under the label of asymmetric regulation[31]. But anyone still seeking to adhere to this should not limit themselves to asking what burdens can be borne by each party. More importantly, they must take the interests of non-participating competitors and users into consideration[32]. And thus we also arrive at an incentive analysis via the backdoor, so to speak. In contrast, we shall in the following allow it to stand at the forefront.

The dispute centers around whether a long-distance network competitor can claim only the switched access to the local network or, alternatively, unbundled access as far back as the bare wires supplied by Deutsche Telekom. We have already emphasized the most important incentive effect of such a claim: it obviates the incentive for competition among networks[33]. The monopolistic bottleneck thus becomes a permanent state of affairs, although it would have disappeared by itself had it not been for the intervention of the regulator.

Additional reasons against extensive unbundling are supplied by institutional economics: namely, that this claim waters down the property rights of the local network[34]. The local network then becomes the servant of three masters. Every change needs the co-operation of Telekom, its long-distance network competitors and the regulatory authority. This reduces the incentive to search for more productive uses of the network, or to expand or develop it, since the watering down of property rights leads to the separation of power and liability. All experience points to the result being paralyzing uncertainty.

Just as difficult is the relationship between Telekom as the network owner and its competitors, to whom it must offer unbundled access. The relationship must be legally understood as a long-term delivery agreement, and not as that found in a society. *Oliver Williamson* has comprehensively examined such agreements[35]. Each of the parties adjusts its dispositions to the continued existence of the agreement. As soon as they have sunk their costs on this basis, the parties slide into a bilateral monopoly. They can both blackmail each other. So that neither side cheats against the other, the parties must provide their relationship with a governance structure. It is also needed because neither can help learning about the other party's business secrets. If Telekom genuinely agrees to unbundled access, its relationship with its competitors must also take into consideration the fact that the demand for telecommunications services changes. In other words, both parties must co-ordinate the planning of the network with each other.

If one takes all this into consideration, it becomes clear that a long-term agreement is, at best, a second-best solution. Much speaks in favor of vertical integration as being more elegant, i.e. saving transaction costs[36]. The legal right to primarily unbundled access would therefore in the long term represent an incentive for Telekom to acquire its competitors, thus achieving the opposite of that desired by the Telecommunications Act.

A last, but no less important, reason for not allowing a right to far-reaching unbundling comes from the field of political economics. Since the incentive to build a network is missing, competitors remain permanently dependent on access to Telekom's networks. Since it cannot be in Telekom's interests to encourage its competitors, these competitors remain permanently dependent on the activity of the regulatory authority. Pointedly, but not exaggeratedly: a right to far-reaching unbundling is a measure that secures the existence of the regulatory authority. This was surely not the intention of the Telecommunications Act.

* I am indebted to *Patricia Adler* for the translation.

[1] See for example *Thomas Lampert*: : Der Begriff der Marktbeherrschung als geeignetes Kriterium zur Bestimmung der Normadressaten für das sektorspezifische Kartellrecht nach dem TKG?, in: WuW 1998, 27 – 38 (36); *Karl-Michael Fuhr/Bärbel Kerkhoff*: Entbündelter Zugang – Vereinbarkeit mit der Eigentumsgarantie des Art. 14 GG ?, in: MMR 1998, 6 – 11 (7).

[2] At any rate, its president *Klaus-Dieter Scheurle* writes: "The creation [sic!] of equal opportunities and functioning competition is the decisive lever also to achieve the other objectives [of the TKG]" (*Klaus-Dieter Scheurle*: Aufgaben der Regulierungsbehörde Telekommunikation und Post, appears in XXXI. FIW-Symposion. Multimedia: Kommunikation ohne Grenzen – grenzenloser Wettbewerb 7, Page 4 of the cover)ft.

[3] Art. 253 ECT (previously Art. 190 ECT).

[4] See § 1 Pharmaceutical Statute or § 1 Statute on Recycling and Waste, for example.

[5] Economically speaking, it concerns the definition of property rights for a private good.

[6] In this context we find that telecommunications services are provided as "private activities" and "the enterprise that was created from the special assets of the Deutsche Bundespost *and* via other private providers" (not emphasised in the original).

[7] One can argue about whether it is a question of distribution policy, or whether the safe provision of telecommunications services to all favored is the concern. In the second case, all favored parties ought to receive just one particular service, whereas in the first case the legislature would thus enjoy more freedom. It would already satisfy its constitutional obligations, if those favored could bring their interest in the service via their willingness to pay in the marketplace. It would suffice, if everyone had an income that allows him to pay for the estimated minimum of telecommunications services.

[8] It is, however, necessary to avoid a misunderstanding. If one formulates the general welfare objective in a less restrictive manner, competition and general welfare no longer stand in opposition to each other. Indeed, competition then becomes the most important instrument with which general welfare is encouraged, since competition theory and system comparisons with liberal telecommunications orders leave no doubt that competition is the superior instrument to give the maximum number of persons access to possibly differentiated telecommunications services at the lowest possible price. A contrast between competition objective and welfare objective only then arises when the state no longer aims for an efficient telecommunications order; and instead aims for certain market results that deviate from an efficient level.

[9] *Hartwig Bartling* summarizes the competition models: Leitbilder der Wettbewerbspolitik. 1980.

[10] Particularly the dispute described under II concerning the access to local loops is formulated in this way.

[11] Details in *Christoph Engel*: Medienordnungsrecht (Law and Economics of International Telecommunications 28) Baden-Baden 1996, 81-97

[12] Institutional economic foundation is found in *Christoph Engel/Günter Knieps*: Die Vorschriften des Telekommunikationsgesetzes über den Zugang zu wesentlichen Leistungen. Eine juristisch-ökonomische Untersuchung (Law and Economics of International Telecommunications 37) Baden-Baden 1998, 77-84; shorter version also under II 4.

[13] Summarised by *Christoph Engel*: Europarechtliche Grenzen für die Industriepolitik, in: *Hans-Werner Rengeling* (ed.): Europäisierung des Rechts (Osnabrücker Rechtswissenschaftliche Abhandlungen 50) 1996, 35 – 67 (42 – 46).

[14] *Martin Cave/Peter Williamson*: Entry, Competition and Regulation in UK Telecommunications, in: Oxford Review of Economic Policy 12 (1996) 100-121 for an overview of developments in England.

[15] *Jean Tirole*: The Theory of Industrial Organization. Cambridge 1988, 239 – 276.

[16] *Günter Knieps*: Phasing Out Sector-Specific Regulation in Competitive Telecommunications, in: Kyklos 50 (1997) 325 – 339.

[17] See also below under c) in regard to substitution competition.

[18] Previously §§ 22 and 26 GWB.

[19] See II below.

[20] More from *Engel/Knieps* (note 12 above) 62 et seq.

[21] More from *Engel/Knieps* (note 12 above) 63 et. seq.

[22] Details in *Engel/Knieps* (note 12 above) 64.

[23] Summarized by *Immenga/Mestmäcker-Immenga* § 1 GWB[2], R 182 et seq.

[24] Details in *Christoph Engel*: Das Völkerrecht des Telekommunikationsvorgangs, in: Rabels Z 1985, 90-120.

[25] Verwaltungsgericht Köln MMR 1998, 102; Oberverwaltungsgericht Münster MMR 1998, 98; Verwaltungsgericht Köln MMR 1999, 13.

[26] The question was the subject of the *Engel/Knieps report* (note 12 above).

[27] See *Engel/Knieps* (note 12 above) 13-32.

[28] A nice portrayal by *Michael Fritsch/Thomas Wein/Hans-Jürgen Ewers:* Marktversagen und Wirtschaftspolitik. Mikroökonomische Grundlagen staatlichen Handelns. Munich[2] 1996, 143-151.

[29] Previously § 26 II GWB.

[30] See only BGH WuW/E 1429, 1432 - Asbach-Fachgroßhändlervertrag; BGH WuW/E 2707, 2716 – Krankentransportunternehmen II.

[31] See above I 3.

[32] More in *Engel/Knieps* (note 12 above) 74-77.

[33] See above I 2.

[34] The writings on the analysis of property rights are extensive. Particularly graphic: *Thráinn Eggertsson*: Economic Behaviour and Institutions (Cambridge Surveys of Economic Literature) 1990, in particular p. 38 et seq.

[35] *Oliver Williamson*: Die ökonomischen Institutionen des Kapitalismus (Die Einheit der Gesellschaftswissenschaften 64) 1990, 77-149.

[36] More on the inner-connection between long-term agreements and vertical integration *Williamson* (note 35 above) 97-116.

3

COSTING AND PRICING IN LIBERALIZED TELECOMMUNICATIONS MARKETS

Günter Knieps
Institute of Transport Economics and Regional Policy
University of Freiburg

I. REGULATORY FRAMEWORK

To fully exploit the potential of competition in liberalized telecommunications markets, the regulatory process should be as lean as possible The application of the disaggregated regulation method, which is characterized by the principles summarized below, is the adequate way to discipline sector-specific market power which still remains [1]:

Minimal regulatory basis

The regulatory basis should not be extended beyond what is absolutely necessary. Thus, measures aimed at disciplining market power should be limited to monopolistic bottleneck areas (local networks). Price and interconnection regulation in the complementary long-distance networks is tantamount to overregulation.

Symmetrical regulation

All active and potential providers of network services must be assured of symmetrical access to the monopolistic bottleneck areas so that (active and potential) competition can develop in full.

The phasing out of sector-specific regulation[2]

The rapid pace of technological progress will lead progressively to an elimination of monopolistic bottleneck areas in the local networks. Consequently, the necessity of regulatory intervention should be reviewed periodically, because once the market power potential has disappeared, the reason for the application of the corresponding regulatory instruments will also cease to exist.

Since the comprehensive opening of the telecommunications market, customer wishes and meeting them efficiently have become the decisive factors. In view of this fact, a symmetrical regulatory framework must be regarded as absolutely necessary. New market entrants should neither be favored nor disadvantaged compared to Deutsche Telekom.

I disagree with the still widespread view that asymmetrical regulation is called for in liberalized telecommunications markets. Regulations that force Deutsche Telekom to offer competitors its interconnection services at extremely low rates (or better yet, free of charge) in order to fulfill the function of a "midwife" for competition are examples of such asymmetrical regulation. Such regulations are not consistent with market conditions and are extraordinarily detrimental to competition. In particular, they run the risk of artificially promoting certain companies or technologies whose superiority in the competitive process has not been established.

II. INFRASTRUCTURE COMPETITION VERSUS SERVICE COMPETITION

The important necessity in competitive telecommunications markets is to provide equal support to service competition and infrastructure competition and not to distort them through regulatory measures. Asymmetrical regulatory requirements that unilaterally inhibit infrastructure competition create the wrong incentives over the long term. The goal must be to create incentives in particular for market entrants to make worthwhile infrastructure investments themselves. A regulation that would require interconnection services to be offered below cost constitutes discrimination against the incumbent network operator. Truly, no one would provide network components voluntarily under such conditions. It can also be assumed that the facilities would never have been built if such regulatory requirements had been taken into consideration ex ante.

The result of asymmetrical regulation imposing disadvantages on the operators of public telecommunications networks would first of all be to create strategic incentives for competitors not to invest, or to invest less, in the construction of their own telecommunications networks; this constitutes a regulatory restraint of infrastructure competition. Furthermore, as demonstrated by the latest controversies, it would create incentives to classify network components as "non-networks."

Moreover, it can be seen that the superfluous regulation of interconnection services in the long-distance area entails further problems associated with regulatory definitions and distinctions that simply do not arise in unregulated markets:

- The problem of defining and distinguishing network operators and operators without their own network is an offshoot of the asymmetrical regulation approach. If the disaggregated regulation method were to be applied, price regulation would be restricted to monopolistic bottleneck areas.

- The overall amount and structure of leased-line rates, as well as the overall amount and structure of interconnection rates or other rates for network access, must be allowed to develop endogenously within the competitive long-distance markets. This eliminates discrimination against the network operator and the attendant incentive distortions.

It follows, therefore, that a precise distinction between network operators and operators without their own network is less important than ensuring that price structures in the telecommunications market be allowed to develop in the process of competition and not be distorted by regulatory interventions.

III. THE GOALS AND METHODS OF RATE REGULATION[3]

Competitive prices between stand-alone costs and short-term marginal costs

A salient feature of the telecommunications sector (even after the full opening of the market) lies in the fact that economies of scope and scale play a significant role in the provision of services. Competitive prices must therefore be allowed to freely find their level between stand-alone costs and short-term marginal costs, depending on demand. An abuse of market power cannot be said to exist in this case. Upper limits for interconnection fees on the basis of uniform mark-ups on incremental costs are not consistent with the new competitive environment. Rather, the short-term marginal costs (variable costs) represent the short-term price floor without constituting predatory pricing. Long-term incremental costs, on the other hand, which also contain the relevant fixed costs, represent the long-term price floor.

Market-oriented allocation of overhead costs

The coverage of product group-specific joint costs and company-specific common costs must be determined in accordance with the prevailing demand conditions (price elasticity of demand). The information required for this purpose is spontaneously generated in the market. Therefore, the resulting allocation of overhead costs may be determined only ex post. Administrative allocation procedures established by the regulator ex ante are fundamentally incapable of anticipating the overhead cost allocation which should be an endogenous result of the market process. The information deficit of the regulatory authorities is too great, especially considering the substantial variation of the relevant demand elasticities over time (time of day, season, etc.).

Price cap regulation and accounting separation

Price cap regulation in the monopolistic bottleneck area and accounting separation are sufficiently capable of disciplining the remaining market power and ensuring the discrimination-free access of service providers in the long-distance markets to the complementary local networks. Detailed input regulation contradicts the spirit of a price cap regulation. One of the main reasons for limiting the scope of regulation to the level of output prices is to keep the information needs of the regulatory authority as low as possible. This will not only reduce regulatory work, but also create entrepreneurial incentives to seek out cost savings and innovative price structures. The decisive advantage of the price cap regulation over the individual rate approval procedure lies in the fact that the former does not impede the entrepreneurial quest for innovative price structures.

Welfare-increasing price differentiation potential

Both at European and national level there is a requirement for discrimination-free access to interconnection services at non-discriminatory prices. These regulations, however, may not be allowed to restrict the diverse welfare-increasing potential of price differentiation in the telecommunications markets.

As already indicated (short-run) variable costs represent the short-term price floor and (long-run) incremental costs the long-term price floor: in addition that both the product group-specific joint costs and the company-specific common costs (overhead costs) must be covered (viability/condition). Therefore a substantial price differentiation potential exists which should be exploited for the benefit of consumers, regardless of the underlying market form selected.[4] In order to evaluate different price differentiation schemes in economic terms, the schemes must be compared in their entirety. It is inadmissible to infer general conclusions about the welfare effects of price differentiation from arbitrary comparisons of individual prices. In particular, a price differentiation required to ensure the survival of the network operator must not be confused with anticompetitive discrimination. In fact, it is the instrument of price differentiation that first allows for undistorted infrastructure and service competition.

The welfare-increasing effects of price differentiation should not be impeded by asymmetrical regulatory intervention. The development of innovative rate structures must be an option open to all providers (Deutsche Telekom and its competitors). One should not hamper the development of new rate structures by extending the requirement for rate approval by the regulatory authority to cover new rates as well. All market participants should have the opportunity of providing optional rates, multiple rates, non-linear price structures, etc. If certain rate models can be offered only by the new market entrants, this would amount to a structural competition restraint on Deutsche Telekom.

IV. COST STUDIES AND COST MODELS AS THE BASIS OF RATE REGULATION

The current debate on cost models for purposes of rate regulation focuses on the costs of efficient service provision. There are considerable differences of opinion not only with respect to the *manner* in which they are determined and documented, but also with respect to the question of *who* can and should determine the costs of efficient service provision.

Criticism of the separation hypothesis

When individual rate approval procedures are applied, as opposed to price cap procedures, the costs of efficient service provision are paramount. The hypothesis that the costs of efficient service provision represent the independent standard by which the actual costs of Deutsche Telekom should be measured has since come to be regarded both by the competitors and the regulatory authority as the accepted interpretation of the legal basis (Telecommunications Act (TKG), Telecommunications Rate Regulation Ordinance (TEntgV))[5].

In the following, I would like to show that this interpretation of the Rate Regulation Ordinance is not only open to question but is also incapable of withstanding a thorough economic analysis.

In competitive telecommunications markets, companies are compelled to make consistent business decisions (regarding investments, product design, pricing, etc.), which in turn is possible only through the consistent use of corporate current cost accounting[6]. As a direct consequence of this fact, the method applied for determining the costs pursuant to Section 2 of the Telecommunications Rate Regulation Ordinance must be such that the figures so produced reflect the costs of efficient service provision as closely as possible. Considering the path dependency of successive network development, the standard applied for regulatory purposes should not be imposed from outside, but developed within the company. It should be mentioned here that the term efficiency is understood in the sense of a "workable efficiency" as opposed to a hypothetical efficiency[7]. Moreover, it always contains a significant dynamic component subject to permanent change. The historical actual costs are not suitable as the standard for regulatory purposes because they are based on information that is no longer relevant to the actual decisions to be taken by the company. Aside from the fact that the reconstruction of historical actual costs for the past is already problematic due to the lack of differentiation, the use of historical costs would lead the company's cost accounting activities in the wrong direction, because the data so determined would neither help the regulatory authority to uncover actual inefficiencies nor help the company to make the right business decisions.

Determination of the decision-relevant costs as the task of the company

In light of the foregoing, one may conclude that there is in fact no objective measure for the determination of efficient costs. The determination of such costs depends in large part on the company's expectations regarding future market trends, technological progress, etc. The formation of such expectations should be left to the company that must also bear the consequences of the decisions made on that basis. A company's current cost accounting supports consistent decision-making on matters involving investments, product design, pricing, etc. and also facilitates transparent cost reporting to the regulator, in the event that such reporting is deemed necessary, for instance in the context of a rate approval procedure.

Ultimately, the determination of the costs of efficient service provision cannot be made by the regulator with the aid of analytical cost models, but represents a genuine task of the respective company.[8] Decisions about pricing, marketing, product design and product range, not to mention investments, are important management decisions that necessarily rely on an effective, decision-oriented cost accounting system to produce the relevant cost information. As a matter of necessity, the company's outlook is future-directed ("forward-looking"), making it necessary to re-evaluate plant and equipment and adjust the economic depreciation in accordance with the market opportunities expected. Competition, changing customer needs and behavior as well as technological progress are factors that constantly influence business decisions with regard to costing and pricing in competitive telecommunications markets.

ENDNOTES

[1] See G. Knieps, The Concept of Open Network Provision in Large Technical Systems, *EURAS Yearbook of Standardization,* Vol 1, 1997, pp. 357-369.

[2] The reader will find a detailed description of the "phasing-out" potential of sector-specific regulation in: G. Knieps, *Phasing Out Sector-Specific Regulation in Competitive Telecommunications,* Kyklos, Vol. 50, Fasc. 3, 1997, pp. 325-339.

[3] See H. Albach, G. Knieps, Kosten und Preise in wettbewerblichen Ortsnetzen ("Costs and Prices in Competitive Local Networks"), Baden-Baden, 1997, p. 18 et seq.

[4] See R.D. Willig, Pareto superior nonlinear outlay schedules, Bell Journal of Economics, Vol. 9, 1978, p. 56-69.

[5] For an illustration of this issue, see p. 343 Schuster/Stürmer, Beck'scher TKG-Kommentar zu §3 TEntgV ("The Becks Telecommunications Act Commentary on Section 3 of the Telecommunications Rate Regulation Ordinance"), in which an explicit distinction is made between the determination of the costs of efficient service provision by the regulatory authority (by application of the benchmarking or engineering approach) and the documentation of the actual costs by the regulated company.

[6] In this regard, see M.A. Salinger, Regulating Prices to Equal Forward-Looking Costs: Cost-Based Prices or Price-Based Costs?, *Journal of Regulatory Economics,* 1998, Vol. 10, pp. 149-163.

[7] See E.G. Furubotn, Economic Efficiency in a World of Frictions, Max Planck Institute for Research into Economic Systems, Discussion Paper 09-98, 1998.

[8] See G. Knieps, Der Irrweg analytischer Kostenmodelle als regulatorische Schattenrechnungen - Eine kritische Analyse der Stellungnahmen zum WIK-Kostenmodell ("The Mistaken Approach of Using Analytical Cost Models as Regulatory Shadow Computations—A Critical Analysis of the Positions Taken on the Cost Model of the "Wissenschaftliches Institut für Kommunikationsdienste"), MultiMedia und Recht, November 1998.

4

REGULATION BY TSLRIC: ECONOMIC EFFECTS ON INVESTMENT AND INNOVATION

Jerry A. Hausman
Massachusetts Institute of Technology

A number of countries have adopted policies to cause dominant network providers to unbundle their networks to provide network elements to new competitors. Two important questions arise with respect to these policies: the degree of network disaggregation that unbundling will cause and the regulated price of the unbundled elements. Economic principles suggest that only the "essential facility" elements of the network, which cannot be economically reproduced in the short term by new competitors, should be unbundled by regulation.[1] It is these essential facility elements that provide the barriers to competition by new entrants. However, if unbundling goes beyond these essential facility elements, new entrants will not have an economic incentive to invest in their own networks. Thus, economic analysis leads to the recommendation that the local network should be unbundled with respect to its essential facility elements, at least in the short run, but that other networks such as long distance and wireless networks should not be unbundled since they do not contain essential facility elements.[2] Overall, long distance and wireless networks should not be regulated so long as competitive entry is sufficient to keep prices at competitive levels.[3]

These economic principles have been recognized by Canadian regulators who require an incumbent local exchange carrier (ILEC) to unbundle its residential loops, but not to unbundle its switching or their transport facilities.[4] Furthermore, the Canadian decision has a sunset provision of 5 years, which is a very desirable attribute to cause new entrants to construct their own networks. To the contrary, the U.S. Federal Communications Commission (FCC) has chosen a high degree of network disaggregation where an ILEC must provide unbundled elements for all services that provides. The FCC did not provide for a sunset provision in its regulation. Thus, the incentive for new competitors to invest in their own networks is significantly less in the U.S. than in Canada.

Most regulatory authorities permitted negotiation between the incumbent provider and the new entrants on the prices of unbundled elements.[5] However, if the parties fail to reach agreement the regulatory authorities will impose price regulation, typically based on a forward looking cost standard. The cost standard used is typically based on the forward looking economic concept of Long Run Incremental Cost (LRIC). The particular standard often used is "Total Service LRIC" (TSLRIC) which also includes the fixed costs associated with the service. Some measure of common costs is often added to the LRIC measure so that the incumbent provider can recover costs not directly attributable to the service.[6]

TSLRIC is an incorrect cost measure to use to set prices for unbundled elements. TSLRIC assumes that cost of investment in telecommunications networks are fixed but not sunk. The reality of telecommunications networks is that much of the investment is sunk and irreversible.[7] For instance, much of the investment in copper or fiber access to residences is likely to be sunk cost because it cannot be redeployed if a substitute technology is used. In telecommunications regulation, a subset of sunk investments are sometimes called potentially stranded assets. Uncertainly has a powerful effect on investment decisions with sunk and irreversible investment, because if demand is not sufficient or prices decrease, the investment will not earn an economic return. To the contrary, if an investment is fixed, but not sunk as assumed by TSLRIC calculations, the asset can always be (costlessly) redeployed and used to provide an alternative service.

I demonstrate in this paper that use of TSLRIC creates negative economic incentives for new investment and for innovation in telecommunications.[8] If the new investment succeeds, the competitors to the incumbent can purchase the unbundled element at cost, as set by TSLRIC. If the new investment does not succeed, the competitor does not bear any of the cost, but the shareholders of the incumbent bear the cost of the unsuccessful investment. Thus, the regulators force the incumbent to provide a *free option* on its investment to its new competitors. Modern economic and finance theory demonstrate the value of options. Regulatory use of TSLRIC causes these free options to be given to new competitors at the expense of the incumbent. The result is a level of investment and innovation by the incumbent below the economically efficient level. New services will then be provided at below economically efficient levels, and consumers and businesses will be made worse off.[9] A markup above TSLRIC is required to provide the correct level of economic incentives for new network investment and innovation. The markup is significant if the proportion of sunk investment in overall investment for a given project is large.

CURRENT FCC APPROACH TO REGULATION OF NEW INVESTMENT IN SERVICES

The U.S. Congress passed the Telecommunications Act of 1996 which was the first basic change in the regulatory framework for telecommunication since 1934. The Congressional legislation called for less regulation, more competition, and the most modern up to date telecommunications infrastructure: "...[T]o provide for a pro-competitive, de-regulatory national policy framework designed to accelerate rapidly private sector deployment of advanced telecommunications and information technologies and services to all Americans by opening all telecommunications markets to competition."[10] The FCC has instituted numerous regulatory rulemakings to implement the 1996 Telecommunication Act. The most important regulations so far have been the Local Competition and Interconnection Order of August 1996.[11] If implemented in its current form, the Local Competition and Interconnection Order will likely have serious negative effects on innovation and new investment in the local telephone network.[12] Similarly, use of TSLRIC-based cost regulation by other countries can also have similar negative effects on innovation and new investment in local telephone networks.

First, I consider the proper goal of regulation set prices in telecommunications. Most economists agree that regulation should be used only when significant market power can lead to unregulated prices well above competitive levels. The goal of regulators is then to set prices at "competitive levels." However, economists are much less explicit about how these competitive levels of prices can be estimated. Most economists would agree that perfect competition cannot yield the appropriate standard since prices set at marginal cost will not allow a privately owned utility to earn a sufficient return on capital to survive. The large fixed costs of telecommunications networks thus do not allow the price equal marginal cost standard of perfect competition to be used.[13]

An alternative competitive standard has been proposed by Prof. Baumol and his co-authors, the "perfect contestability" standard. Prof. Baumol has proposed that the regulators should require firms to set prices as if "the competitive pressures generated by fully unimpeded and costless entry and exit, contrary to fact, were to prevail."[14] However, costless entry and exit presumes that no sunk costs exist, i.e. costs that cannot be recovered upon exit by a firm. This assumption of no sunk costs is extremely far from economic and technological reality in telecommunications where the essence of most investments is an extremely high proportion of sunk costs. Consider the investment by an incumbent local exchange carrier (ILEC) in a new local fiber optic network which can provide new broadband services and high speed internet access to residential customers. Most of the investment is sunk since if the broadband network does not succeed, the investment cannot be recovered. Thus, when either technological or economic uncertainty exists "perfect contestability as a generalization of perfect competition" cannot provide the correct competitive standard.

In a perfectly contestable market, if the return to an investment decreases below the competitive return, the investment is immediately removed from the market and used elsewhere. This costless exit strategy is always available in a perfectly contestable market. However, the actual economics of telecommunications investment could not be further from a perfectly contestable market. When fiber optic networks are constructed, they are in large part sunk investments.[15] If their economic return falls below competitive levels, the firm cannot shift them to other uses because of their sunk and irreversible nature.[16] Thus, the use of a perfectly contestable market standard fails to recognize the important feature of sunk and irreversible investments—they eliminate costless exit. Because of its failure to take into account the sunk and irreversible nature of investments, the contestable market model has nothing of interest to say about competition in telecommunications. An industry cannot be expected to behave in a manner that is fundamentally inconsistent with its underlying technological and economic characteristics.

One way to consider the problem is the situation of a new investment by an ILEC. Suppose a competitor wants to buy the unbundled elements associated with the investment. The ILEC could offer the new competitor a contract for the economic life of the investment—say 10 years for investment in the local loop. The price of the unbundled element would be the total investment cost plus the operating costs each year for the unbundled element. If demand did not materialize or prices fell, the new entrant would bear the economic risk of this outcome.[17] However, regulation by TSLRIC typically allows the new entrant to buy the use of the unbundled element on a month-

trant to buy the use of the unbundled element on a month-by-month basis. Thus if demand does not materialize or prices fall, the ILEC has to bear the risk for the business case of the new competitor. Thus, the ILEC has been required by regulation to give a *free option* to the new entrant, where an option is the right but not the obligation to purchase the use of the unbundled elements. The monthly price of the unbundled element should be significantly higher than the 10 year price of the element to reflect the risk inherent in the sunk investments, or equivalently the value of the option given to the new entrant.[18] Regulators to date have not incorporated the value of the option into their price setting.

Another way to consider the problem of regulation set prices is to allow for the existence of the (all-knowing) social planner. Suppose the social planner were considering a new investment in a telecommunications network where the features of sunk and irreversible investments is important. The social planner wants to maximize the value of the social welfare integral over time subject to uncertainty. However, the investment is subject to both technological and economic uncertainty so that the cost of the investment may (randomly) decrease in the future and because of demand uncertainty the social planner does not know whether the investment will be economic. In making an optimal decision the social planner will take into account the sunk and irreversible nature of the investment since if the new service fails, the investment cannot be shifted to another use. Thus, assuming that sunk costs do not exist, which is the perfect contestability standard, when sunk costs are an extremely important part of the economic problem will lead to incorrect decisions and decreased economic efficiency. The economy will not reach its production possibility frontier.

REGULATION SET PRICES FOR UNBUNDLED ELEMENTS

Under the Telecommunication Act of 1996 the FCC mandated forward looking cost based prices for competitors to use unbundled LEC facilities.[19] The FCC did not permit any markup over cost to allow for the risk associated with investment in sunk assets; instead, it used a TSLRIC type approach that attempts to estimate the total service long run incremental cost on a forward looking basis.[20] TSLRIC attempts to solve the perfect competition problem that price cannot equal marginal cost by allowing for the fixed costs of a given service to be recovered. TSLRIC allows for recovery of the cost of investment and variable costs of providing the service over the economic lifetime of the investment. However, TSLRIC makes no allowance for the sunk and irreversible nature of telecommunications investment, so that it adopts the perfect contestability standard. The perfect contestability standard provides the incorrect economic incentives for efficient investment once technological and economic uncertainty exist. The FCC has chosen the incorrect standard for setting regulated prices. TSLRIC will lead to less innovation and decreased investment below economically efficient levels.

The TSLRIC Standard and R&D and Investment in New Services

The first and easiest example that I consider is R&D and investment in new services. Many new telecommunications services do not succeed, as recent failures include Picturephone services (AT&T and MCI within the past eight years) and information service gateway services offered by many ILECs. These new gateway services required substantial sunk costs of development because creation of the large data bases to provide information service gateways is substantial. Now if a new service is successful, under TSLRIC regulation, an ILEC competitor can buy the service at TSLRIC. Thus, for a successful new service the ILEC recovers at most its cost. For unsuccessful services, the ILEC recovers nothing and loses its sunk investment. Thus, the

TSLRIC regulation is the analogue of a rule which would require pharmaceutical companies to sell their successful products to their generic competitors at incremental cost and would allow the pharmaceutical companies to recover their R&D and production costs on their successful new drugs, but to recover nothing on their unsuccessful attempts.

This truncation of returns where a successful new telecommunications service recovers its cost (but no more), and unsuccessful new services recover nothing decreases economic incentives for innovative new services from regulated telecommunications companies. By eliminating the right tail of the distribution of returns as demonstrated in Figure 1, TSLRIC regulation decreases the mean of the expected return of a new project. For example, consider a project with returns, y, which follow a normal distribution with mean μ and standard deviation σ, the expected value of the return when it is truncated at cost c is:

$$E(y \mid y < c) = \mu - \sigma M(c) \tag{1.1}$$

where M(c) is the inverse Mills ratio evaluated at c.[21] Thus, the tighter is the cost standard, the lower are the incentives to innovate, as expected. More importantly, note that as the returns to the innovation

Figure 1.

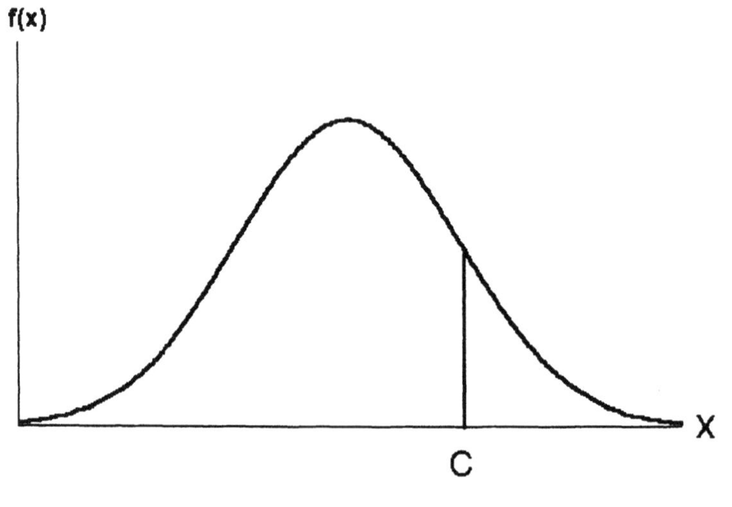

become more uncertain, the expected return and the incentives to innovate also decrease. Thus, even in the absence of sunk and irreversible investments, a TSLRIC pricing policy will decrease the economic incentives for investment in innovative services, and a TSLRIC policy may eliminate these economic incentives to invest altogether.

Regulators could allow for something similar to patent protection for new services to provide economic incentives for ILECs to innovate.[22] However, this policy option is a recipe to hold up new telecommunications services for ten years or more with enormous consumer welfare losses as occurred with voice messaging and cellular telephone.[23] Currently, it takes the U.S. Patent Office over two years to grant a patent with longer time periods not uncommon. However, no opponent of the patent is allowed to be part of the process. In a regulatory setting where competitors would attempt to delay the introduction of new services as happened with both voice messaging and cellular telephone, I would expect much longer delays. Thus, the patent approach will not solve the problem. A better approach would be not to regulate new services. Given the large welfare gains from new services and price cap regulation for existing services, ILECs should be permitted to offer new services with no prior approval or price regulation. The gains in consumer welfare from successful new services would lead to significant gains for consumers. Attempting to "fine tune" prices of new services through cost based regulation will lead to overall consumer losses. However, regulators find it extremely difficult not to regulate any new service of a regulated company.

The Effect of Sunk and Irreversible Investments[24]

TSLRIC assumes that all capital invested now will be used over the entire economic life of the new investment and that prices for the capital goods or the service being offered will not decrease over time. With changing demand conditions, changing prices, or changing technology, these assumptions are not necessarily true. Thus, TSLRIC assumes a world of certainty where the actual world is one of uncertainty in the future. Significant economic effects can arise from the effects that the sunk nature of investment has on the calculation of TSLRIC.

Consider the value of a project under no demand uncertainty with a risk adjusted discount rate of r and assumed known exponential economic depreciation at rate δ. This assumption on depreciation can be thought of as the price of the capital decreasing over time at this rate due to technological progress. Assume that price, net of the effect of economic depreciation of the capital goods, is expected to decrease with growth rate $-\alpha$.[25] The initial price of output is P. The value of the project is:

$$V(P) = \int_0^\infty \lambda \exp(-\lambda t)\, P \frac{1 - \exp(-\delta t)}{\delta} dt = P/(\lambda + \delta) \qquad (1.2)$$

where $\lambda = r + \alpha$. Note that δ is added to expression to account for the decreasing price of capital goods. This term, omitted from TSLRIC calculations, accounts for technological progress in equipment prices, which is one economic factor that leads to lower prices over time. Suppose that the cost of the investment is I. The rule for a competitive firm is to invest if $V(P) > I$. Equivalently from equation (1.2), $P > (\lambda + \delta)\, I$. The economic interpretation of this expression is that the price (or price minus variable cost) must exceed the cost of capital, which includes the change in price of the capital good to make the investment worthwhile.[26] Note that the net change in the output price and the price of the capital good both enter the efficient investment rule. TSLRIC calculations ignore the basic economic fact that when technological change is present, (quality adjusted) capital goods prices tend to decline over time. This economic factor needs to be taken into account or economic inefficiency will result. Furthermore, regulators should set realistic depreciation lives for telecommunications investment. In a competitive environment unrealistically long depreciation lives create economic disincentives for new investment by regulated companies because they will not recover a significant proportion of their investment.

Now, a TSLRIC calculation does not include δ, but it instead assumes that the price of capital goods does not change over time. This assumption is extremely inaccurate. Take a Class 5 Central Office Switch (COS) for example. Ten years ago an AT&T Class 5 switch (5-ESS) was sold to an ILEC for approximately $200 per line (Hausman and Kohlberg (1989), p. 204). Today, the price of AT&T 5-ESS switches and similar NTI switches are in the $70 per line or lower range. A TSLRIC calculation would be based on the $70 price. An ILEC who paid $200 per line made the efficient investment decision when it purchased its COS. But TSLRIC, by omitting economic depreciation due to technological progress, leads to a systematically downward biased estimate of costs. Indeed, I estimate the economic depreciation of central office switches to be near 8% per year over the past five years, while the cost of fiber optic carrier systems has decreased at approximately 7% per year over the same period. The omitted economic factor δ can be quite large relative to r for telecommunications switching or transmission equipment due to technological progress.

TSLRIC calculations makes the following further assumptions: (1) the investment is used at full capacity always, (2) the demand curve does not shift inwards over time, and (3) a new technology does not appear that leads to lower cost of production. Of course, these conditions are unlikely to hold true over the life of the sunk investment. Thus uncertainty needs to be added to the calculation because of the sunk nature of the investment.

I now account for the sunk nature of the investment and its interaction with fundamental economic and technological uncertainty. Given the fundamental uncertainty and the sunk nature of the investment, a "reward for waiting" occurs because over time some uncertainty is resolved. The uncertainty can arise from at least 4 factors: (1) Demand uncertainty, (2) Price uncertainty, (3) Technological progress (input price) uncertainty, and (4) Interest rate uncertainty.[27] Now the fundamental decision rule for investment changes to:

$$P^s > \frac{\beta_1}{\beta_1 - 1}(\delta + \lambda)I \tag{1.3}$$

where $\beta_1 > 1$ so that $m = \beta_1/(\beta_1 - 1) > 1$. The parameter β_1 takes into account the sunk cost nature of the investment coupled with inherent economic uncertainty.[28] Parameter m is the mark-up factor required to account for the effect of uncertain economic factors on the cost of sunk and irreversible investments. Thus, the critical cut off point for investment is $P^S > P$ from equation (1.2).

To see how important this consideration of sunk costs can be, I evaluate the markup factor m. The parameters β_1 and m depend on a number of economic factors. It can be demonstrated that as uncertainty increases, i.e. the variance of the underlying stochastic process, β_1 decreases and the m factor increases. Also, as δ increases, β_1 increases which means that the m factor decreases. As r increases β_1 decreases so that the m factor increases. MacDonald and Siegel (1986) and Dixit and Pindyck (1994, p.153) calculate m = 2 so that, for instance, V^S = 2I. A TSLRIC calculation which ignores the sunk cost feature of telecommunications network investments would thus be off by a factor of two.

Using parameters for ILECs and taking account of the decrease in capital prices due to technological progress (which Dixit and Pindyck assume to be zero in their calculation) and because the expected change in (real) prices of most telecommunications services is also negative given the decreasing capital prices, I calculate the value of m to be around 3.2-3.4.[29] Thus, a markup factor must be applied to the investment cost component of TSLRIC to account for the interaction of uncertainty with sunk and irreversible costs of investment.[30] Depending on the ratio of sunk costs to fixed and variable costs the overall markup on TSLRIC will vary, but the markup will be significant given the importance of sunk costs in most telecommunications investments. Note that this same markup over TSLRIC would be used by the hypothetical social planner to choose optimal investment in a telecommunications network since the social planner would face the same inherent economic and technological uncertainty over future demand and cost factors.

Now when the markup for sunk and irreversible investment is applied, it should only be used for assets which are sunk, e.g. potentially stranded. Other investments that are fixed, but not sunk, would not have the markup. I have applied this methodology to links and ports, which are treated as unbundled elements by U.S. regulation. The proportion for sunk costs for links is 0.59 so that the markup factor for the overall investment using a markup factor of m = 3.3 is approximately 2.35 times TSLRIC. By contrast, the proportion of sunk costs for ports is about 0.10 so that the markup factor becomes 1.23 times TSLRIC. The markup over TSLRIC that takes account of sunk costs and uncertainty is the value of the free option that regulators force incumbent providers to grant to new entrants; e.g. 1.35 times TSLRIC for links and 0.23 times TSLRIC for ports. Thus, the proportion of sunk costs has an important effect on the correct value of regulated prices when sunk costs are taken into account.

Regulators, by failing to apply a markup to TSLRIC, will set too low a regulated price for telecommunications services from new investment. The result will be to decrease new investment in telecommunications below economically efficient levels, contrary to the stated purpose of the Telecommunications Act of 1996 in the U.S. and enabling legislation in other countries. Thus, through its focus on static cost efficiency considerations in setting regulated prices equal to TSLRIC, the regulators will miss the negative effect on dynamic efficiency that TSLRIC-based prices will cause. Since the examples of voice messaging, cellular telephone, and the Internet demonstrate that the dynamic efficiency effects are quite large in telecommunications, use of TSLRIC to set regulated prices will likely cause substantial welfare losses to consumers similar to past FCC regulatory policy in the U.S.

CONCLUSIONS

Cost based regulation of telecommunications (e.g. rate of return regulation in the U.S.) had significant negative effects on innovation while it was claimed that it led to excessive capital investment. Most economists decided that cost based regulation led to significant consumer harm. During the 1980s price cap regulation replaced cost based regulation in many countries. Price cap regulation has important economic incentive attributes for innovation and investment in telecommunications networks by the incumbent firm.

During the 1990s cost based regulation has reappeared because of the necessity to set price for unbundled network elements sold by incumbent firms to their competitors. Unfortunately, the adoption of TSLRIC as a cost basis to set the prices for unbundled elements has negative economic incentive effects for innovation and for new investment in telecommunications networks. Failure by regulators to recognize the sunk cost character of much network investment leads to the grant of a free option to the competitors of the incumbent. Causing the shareholders of the incumbent firm to fund the free option for the competition will lead to underinvestment. Given the amount of uncertainty in a dynamic industry with rapidly changing technology and economics can have an especially large effect on investment incentives because the value of the option is high. The loses will be consumers and businesses who will not have access to the most up to date service that would be provided if regulatory did not create disincentives to new investment.

REFERENCES

Baumol W. J. and J. G. Sidak, *Toward Competition in Local Telephony*, MIT Press, 1994,

Dixit, A. And R. Pindyck, *Investment Under Uncertainty*, Princeton Univ. Press, 1994.

Farrell, J., "Competition, Innovation and Deregulation," mimeo, 1997.

Hausman, J., "Competition in Long Distance and Equipment Markets: Effects of the MFJ," *Journal of Managerial and Decision Economics*, 1995.

Hausman, J., "Reply Affidavit of Prof. Jerry Hausman," FCC CC Docket No. 96-98, July 1996, mimeo.

Hausman, J., "Valuation and the Effect of Regulation on New Services in Telecommunications," *Brookings Papers on Economic Activity: Microeconomics*, 1997.

Hausman, J., "Telecommunications: Building the Infrastructure for Value Creation," in S. Bradley and R. Nolan eds., *Sense and Respond*, Harvard Business School Press, 1998.

Hausman J. and W. E. Kohlberg, "The Evolution of the Central Office Switch Industry," in S. Bradley and J. Hausman eds., *Future Competition in Telecommunications*, Harvard Business School Press, 1989.

Hausman, J. and T. Tardiff, "Efficient Local Exchange Competition," *Antitrust Bulletin*, 1995.

Kahn, A.E., *The Economics of Regulation*, Cambridge: MIT Press, 1988.

Laffont, J.J. and J. Tirole, "Competition in Telecommunications," mimeo, Nov. 1996.

MacDonald R. and D. Siegel , "The Value of Waiting to Invest," *Quarterly Journal of Economics*, 101, 707–728, 1986.

Schafer H., *Telecommunications Law*, RWS Verlag Kommunikationsforum, 1998

ENDNOTES

[1] See J. Hausman and T. Tardiff, "Efficient Local Exchange Competition," *Antitrust Bulletin*, 1995 for further economic analysis. The "essential facility" elements are also referred to as "monopoly building blocks".

[2] Indeed, my academic research demonstrates that regulation of cellular telephone and long distance led to *higher* prices to consumers in the U.S. due to the signaling function of required tariff filings that decreased competition. Prices in both cellular and long distance decreased after the tariff regulation was eliminated.

[3] Claims that regulation is required to keep prices from becoming "too low" from possible predatory pricing are incorrect and cause consumer harm from higher prices. Predatory pricing in long distance or wireless networks is extremely unlikely since it is not economically rational business behavior as I discuss in Hausman (1995).

[4] CRTC "Local Competition", Telecom Decision CRTC 97-8, May 1, 1997.

[5] This procedure has been adopted in the U.S., Australia, and Germany. For the description of the German framework, see Dr. Helge Schafer, *Telecommunications Law*, RWS Verlag Kommunikationsforum, 1998.

[6] For instance in Canada, a markup of 25% over TSLRIC is used.

[7] Economists refer to a cost as sunk when the investment cannot be re-used or sold, except at a significant loss, if the firm exits the business.

[8] See Hausman (1998) for a discussion of the important gains that have been realized by innovation in the Internet.

[9] For a discussion and estimation of particular cases where regulation cost U.S. consumers and businesses billions of dollars due to regulatory delay of new services, see J. Hausman,

"Valuation and the Effect of Regulation on New Services in Telecommunications," *Brookings Papers on Economic Activity: Microeconomics,* 1997.

10. Conference Report to the Telecommunications Act of 1996, S. 652.

7' FCC, "First Report and Order, CC docket No. 96-98 and 95-185," August 1, 1996.

12. The FCC is being challenged by the incumbent local exchange carriers (ILECs) in Federal Court. The case has been heard, but not yet decided, by the U.S. Supreme Court. Two issues are under consideration: whether the FCC has improperly usurped the rights of states to set regulated rates for local competition and the pricing framework used to set these rates. I only consider the latter issue here.

13 Economists have long agreed on this point. See e.g. Kahn (1988) for a discussion.

14. W. J. Baumol and J. Gregory Sidak (1994), p. 28. and pp. 31 ff.

15 The electronic used in the networks need not be sunk, but much of the actual dark fiber will be a sunk investment.

16. This feature of sunk and irreversible investment has been widely recognized by economic research in the past 10 years. See MacDonald and Siegel (1986) and for a recent comprehensive textbook treatment see Dixit and Pindyck (1994).

17 The contract (or regulation) could allow the new entrant to sell the use of the unbundled element to another firm if it decided to exit the business.

18 In contracts between unregulated telecommunications companies, e.g. long distance carriers, and their customers, significant discounts are given for multi-year contracts.

19. The FCC decision is currently under appeal. In the FCC proceeding I provided testimony on behalf of the ILECs.

20. The FCC chose a variant of TSLRIC, called TELRIC for total element LRIC. However, the essential economic problem of TSLRIC also exists in TELRIC. The FCC is currently constructing a TELRIC model to be used in future regulatory proceedings.

21. The inverse Mills ratio is the ratio of the density function and distribution function of the standard normal distribution evaluated at $(c - \mu)/\sigma$. The inverse Mills ration M(C) increases monotonically as c decrease for given μ and σ.

22. The FCC chief economist, Dr. Joseph Farrell (1997) considered this option.

23 See J. Hausman, op.cit., for a discussion for consumer losses from this policy.

24. This discussion follows Hausman (1996). See also Laffont and Tirole (1996).

25. This factor arises due to changes in demand and changes in total factor productivity.

26. For simplicity, I am assuming only capital costs and no variable costs in this calculation. Variable costs can be included by reinterpreting P to be price minus variable costs which will lead to the same solution.

27. The FCC incorrectly assumed that taking account of *expected* price changes in capital goods and economic depreciation is sufficient to estimate the effect of changing technology and demand conditions; see the FCC "First Report and Order", para. 686. Thus, the FCC implicitly assumed that the variances of the stochastic processes which determine the uncertainty are zero, e.g. that no uncertainty exists. Under the FCC approach the values of all traded options should be zero (contrary to stock market fact), since the expected price change of the underlying stock does not enter the option value formula. It is the uncertainty related to the stochastic process as well as the time to expiration which gives value to the option as all option pricing formulae demonstrate, e.g. the Black-Scholes formula.

28. I do not derive this equation here since it is the solution to a differential equation. For a derivation see e.g. Dixit and Pindyck (1994), pp. 254-256 pp. 279-280, and p. 369. The parameter β_1 depends on the expected risk adjusted discount rate of r, expected exponential economic depreciation δ, and the net expected price $-\alpha$, and the amount of uncertainty in the underlying stochastic process. Note that this result holds under imperfect competition, not just under monopoly, as some critics have claimed incorrectly.

29. Because of the expected decrease in the price of capital goods, even if the standard deviation of the underlying stochastic process were 0.25 as high as a typical stock, the markup factor would still be 2.1. For a standard deviation 0.5 as high, the markup factor is 2.4. I have also explored the effect of the finite expected economic lifetimes of the capital investments in telecommunications infrastructure. Using expect lifetimes of 10-15 years leads to only small changes in the option value formulas, e.g. for a project with a 12 year economic life the markup factor of 2.0 changes to 1.9.

30. It is the advent of competition which requires correct regulatory policy to apply the markup. Previously, when regulatory policy did not allow for competition, regulators could (incorrectly) set prices based on historic capital costs. Given the onset of competition arising from the 1996 Telecommunication Act and regulatory removal of barriers to competition, regulators must now account for changes in prices over time. Otherwise, ILECs will decrease their investment below economically efficient levels because their expected returns, adjusted for risk, will be too low to justify the new investment.

5

WHAT IS WRONG WITH AMERICAN TELECOMMUNICATIONS?

Paul W. MacAvoy
Yale School of Management

J. Gregory Sidak
American Enterprise Institute

For more than sixty years, voice telephony was provided by the American Telephone and Telegraph Company (AT&T) as the franchised and regulated monopoly. Divested of its local operating companies in the 1984 landmark antitrust case, AT&T has become the dominant of three voice and data long distance providers while its former operating companies have become dominant single providers of local service. After nearly three years of telecommunications explicit "deregulation" in the United States, centering on the Telecommunication Act of 1996, there is little to which regulatory officials in charge of such deregulation can point in terms of benefits in the form of lower prices or innovative services. The prospects for rapid improvement are bleak. Whether or not America's defectively designed regulatory institutions are reparable, it is critical that other nations recognize the

American mistakes in telecommunications and strive to avoid repeating them.

The "star" network configuration required for provision of telecommunications services has inherent economics of scope and scale, as well as well-recognized network externalities. These structural characteristics have attracted regulation, in the form of state and federal agencies that determine the holder of a "franchise" and the terms and condition for the franchises to provide service. Regulation of telecommunications in the United States has been embodied in a "regulatory contract" between the private carrier and the regulatory authority, which in the first instance is a state public utilities commission (PUC) and in the second instance is the Federal Communications Commission (FCC), which has jurisdiction over interstate communications. In practice, American regulators have shaped the regulatory contract in a manner that sacrifices the economies of scale and scope; instead they have designed the regulatory contract to capture network externalities and to use supracompetitive returns on exclusive service provision to fund various politically favored goals.

American telecommunications contains an artificial regulatory segregation of local exchange telephony from interexchange ("long-distance") telephony that arose principally from the manner in which the U.S. Department of Justice and AT&T settled their antitrust lawsuit with the divestiture of the Bell System in 1984. This distinction is important because it affects in substantially different ways the competitive strategies of the local exchange carriers and the interexchange carriers. The adverse unintended consequences of the divestiture decree would, after the Telecommunications Act of 1996, be little more than a historical curiosity were it not for the fact that the 1996 legislation enshrined much of the misguided case-by-case policy that arose between 1984 and 1996. Foremost among the consequences has been an application of regulatory and antitrust policy that has perpetuated barriers to entry into interexchange markets on the basis of an American version of dominant firm regulation.

In addition, incumbent local exchange carriers (known as ILECs under the Telecommunications Act of 1996) face a regulatory disadvantage. Where the state public utilities commissions (PUCs) have promoted entry, principally in commercial and industrial services, the ILECs seek to match the prices and services of entrants (known as competitive local exchange carriers or CLECs). But in low-density residential and small business markets, the ILECs have recently sought to set higher prices, now free of subsidies, and high enough to equal to the stand-alone cost of service by potential entrants (namely, the CLECs). This reversal of sectoral price levels—now low on industrial, high on residential—has been a restructuring that has followed behind market changes. Beyond playing catch-up, the ILECs seek to develop new profit opportunities by bundling local exchange and local interexchange services with long-distance services. But all of the regional Bell operating companies (RBOCs), which notably do not include GTE, continue as of the end of 1998 to be unable to obtain FCC certification to offer customers bundled service in their local service regions.

The basic determinant of the competitive condition of the ILECs has been a set of regulatory policies concerning entry and its consequences for cost recovery of the incumbent telephony network. These policies seek to achieve an overlay by entrants on the incumbent star network of the local loop, central office switch, trunk/tandem, to terminal or long distance switch. The FCC seeks at least a partial new layer, with the old and new interconnected, before declaring local exchange to be "competitive." Only achieving that designation allows the incumbent carrier to become an entrant in other more profitable markets (such as long distance). With respect to entry, the regulator may accomplish the pricing of unbundled network elements (UNEs) in either of two ways: The regulator can price UNEs on the basis of efficiency principles, or the regulator can provide the entrant an implicit subsidy, by implementation of "TELRIC plus X" prices, where TELRIC denotes total element long-run incremental cost. The adoption of the latter pricing rule to date, which is widespread at the state level, has created a stand-off between ILECs and entrants. That impasse has prevented the telecommunications industry from restructuring on the basis of economic efficiency rather than regulatory strategy. Surely it is economic folly to mandate unbundling of any network element that is not "essential" in the antitrust sense—that is, a network element that cannot be readily duplicated by the entrant or procured at competitive prices from the same vendors who supply the element to the incumbent firm subject to the unbundling obligation.

The impasse over pricing of unbundled network access also has induced the ILECs to resort to constitutional litigation that asserts that regulators have set TELRIC in a way that produces prices and terms for unbundling that are inherently uncompensatory. Consequently, they argue, the rules for pricing UNEs confiscate an ILEC's property without just compensation. This gives rise to claims for "stranded costs," currently one of the most controversial subjects in the regulation of network industries.

Stranded costs are costs that a regulated firm has been authorized to recover through regulated prices, but which the firm is no longer able to recover once the market in which it provides service is open to competition. One can envision at least three kinds of stranded costs.

In the United States the kind of stranded cost that is most familiar is in the electricity context, and these are what might be called "historic" stranded costs. Such costs are associated with nuclear plants, renewable energy contracts, and other currently uneconomic investments for the supply of electricity that were made in the past. The recovery of the cost of, and a competitive return on, that investment was designed to take place over an extended period of years, through depreciation schedules. But the advent of competition occurs before full cost recovery has taken place. Some in the United States doubt the existence of a stranded cost problem in telecommunications because they do not observe similar kinds of uneconomic historic investments in capacity. That view, however, ignores that *any* kind of investment in capacity may be rendered uneconomic if it has been subject to cost recovery at an allowed rate of regulatory depreciation that lags behind the true rate of economic depreciation.

A second kind of stranded cost is what might be called "forward-looking" stranded cost. This problem is especially critical in the American telecommunications industry. It arises where the current structure of regulated retail rates is such that when the network is unbundled and pieces of the network are priced on an incremental cost basis (or even below an incremental cost basis, as we believe to be the case in some states). In this circumstance, there is a revenue shortfall that is incurred each day the incumbent firm operates under those price regulations. That is a revenue shortfall that continues into the future. Unlike historic stranded costs, these forward-looking stranded costs are not the least bit retrospective in nature.

A third kind of stranded cost, also prospective in nature, can arise if, after the move to open network access, the incumbent firm continues to bear asymmetric regulatory obligations, such as carrier of last resort obligations or requirements to provide service to certain preferred customer classes below the true cost of providing service to those customers. As selective entry takes place and picks off the high-margin customers who provide the source of funds to subsidize those negative-margin activities, there is a revenue shortfall. Again, this cost recovery shortfall takes place each day into the future that the incumbent firm operates under that regulatory structure.

This form of targeted entry is often called "cherry picking" or "cream skimming." The term that has been coined to describe the circumstances that give rise to vulnerability to cherry picking or cream skimming is "incumbent burdens." An incumbent burden is the opposite of a barrier of entry. It is a burden that is asymmetrically borne by an incumbent firm but not the entrant. So, when the entrant arrives, that firm does not face that cost when competing against the regulated firm that is already serving the entire market.

There are three basic scenarios by which the stranded cost issue has been addressed by regulatory bodies in actual cases in the United States and elsewhere. The first is the Hong Kong experience, which, to our knowledge, has not been followed so far in the United States. In late 1997 and early 1998, the Office of Telecommunications Authority in Hong Kong wanted Hong Kong Telecom, which had an exclusive international license that was set to expire early in the next century, to relinquish prematurely its license and thus forfeit its exclusivity. In Hong Kong, because of the small size of the area, there are only two kinds of service: local service and international. There is no service akin to domestic long distance. Thus, the international license generated all the revenue that Hong Kong Telecom used to subsidize monthly local rates for both residential customers and business customers in Hong Kong. In the span of about three months, the regulator and the company negotiated a resolution of the stranded cost problem that consisted of the following terms. Hong Kong Telecom agreed to surrender its exclusivity. In return, the regulator allowed Hong Kong Telecom to rebalance rates, bringing business customers' rates immediately up to cost and residential customers' monthly access rates up to cost over a three-year phase-in period. In addition, when the parties then calculated the remaining net revenue impact of the loss of exclusivity, it was clear that there was still a shortfall. So the government of Hong Kong wrote a check to Hong Kong Telecom for about U.S.$800 million. To our knowledge, there has not been any similar experience in the United States of a regulator and the incumbent firm swiftly negotiating a deal for addressing stranded costs.

The second approach to stranded cost issues is one where regulators either have (1) rejected the idea that there is such a thing as stranded costs that gives the regulated firm a legally enforceable right against the government or (2) disputed the magnitude of stranded costs to such an extent that the practical effect is to reject any appreciable recovery. In those cases, the result has been litigation by the incumbent regulated firm against the public utility commission for violation of the Takings Clause of the Fifth Amendment of the U. S. Constitution and also for breach of the regulatory contract. This litigation approach to stranded cost recovery has played out in electric power in New Hampshire. In telecommunications, takings claims have been pressed by GTE and other companies in dozens of states based on the belief that the regulated prices of unbundled network elements were set at confiscatory levels. Also in the appeals of FCC orders relating to unbundling of network elements, access charge reform, and universal service reform, telephone companies and their trade association, the U.S. Telephone Association, have pressed takings arguments to the U.S. Courts of Appeals.

The third approach to addressing stranded cost issues is the route that Massachusetts, Pennsylvania, California and other states have chosen in their restructuring of the electric power industry. This process brings all the stakeholders get together, usually in a very expansive notice of proposed rulemaking. Public comment is solicited on a wide range of issues—not just stranded cost issues, but also codes of conduct, supplier of last resort obligation, and so forth. Such a proceeding has generally followed the enactment of a retail competition statute by the state legislature, or in some cases it may anticipate enactment of such a statute. In these states, it has been recognized that once retail competition is permitted, the price of retail services is no longer a viable means to recover stranded costs; thus, stranded costs must be recovered through a non-bypassable, competitively neutral end-user charge. That charge goes on the bill of all electricity customers, and thus it does not affect the choice of whether a customer buys electricity from *A* or *B*. The charge resembles the subscriber line charge in telecommunications.

One clever variation on the end-user charge is to "securitize" the stranded costs. This is done through the issuance of "transition bonds." The amount of stranded costs that has been estimated and approved for recovery is paid off immediately through a bond issuance that is serviced by an end-user charge known as the "transition bond charge." This approach that has been taken in Pennsylvania in the electric power industry. It has the effect of placing the cost recovery risk on new investors who step into the shoes of the investors of the incumbent utility. These bond issuances are expected to be AAA-rated because they are relatively secure debt instruments. Even though the bonds are not backed by the full faith and credit of the state, they are serviced exclusively by a rate order that is approved by the regulator specifically for that purpose.

The dilemma of stranded cost recovery in American telecommunications could, of course, have been averted through the adoption of an alternative regulatory strategy that would not have attempted to set UNE prices at all, but rather would have opened all markets to competitive entry. Regulators have rejected that approach because certain potentially adverse regulatory consequences can be envisioned. Thus, the FCC defines the terms of the debate at a level of abstract, conjectural meta-reality. The debate takes on a life of its own, with entrants and incumbents expected to frame their strategies in terms of effects on abstract results that the FCC focuses on. One finds, for example, respected scholars advocating elaborate tests for determining the permissible date for market entry by the RBOCs into long-distance markets. It is inherent in the FCC's meta-reality that the agency's fears of potential long distance competitive harms cannot be falsified. In this respect, the FCC's fears are self-fulfilling prophecies of the need for continued regulatory oversight of entry into all markets.

Unfortunately, the official policy of the United States during the current administration appears to be to export America's approach to telecommunications regulation to every nation seeking in wonderment to appreciate it. This orientation is clear from the way that the FCC attempted to put its gloss on the 1997 World Trade Organization (WTO) agreement on telecommunications services and, in particular, the way in which the FCC has attempted to dictate to other sovereign nations the terms of reform of settlement rates while ignoring the pricing of U.S. outbound international services. Similarly, with respect to pricing of unbundled network elements, one should expect that in other nations that are signatories to the 1997 WTO agreement on telecommunications services, pricing that follows TELRIC rules for UNEs will be the central, and most disruptive issue to be resolved in implementing "procompetitive regulatory principles" outlined in the WTO's reference paper.

What is the escape from this situation, in which industry growth is held back by the lack of competitive entry brought about by regulatory agencies ostensibly acting in the name of protecting consumers? It is natural to fall back on the standard *deus ex machina* of technological innovation. To be sure, there are technologies that offer bypass of the stalemate, such as internet telephony for long-distance. These responses, however, can go a great deal further than just equipment replacement. In response to the perverse regulatory environment that has evolved since 1996, one can envision "the strategic corporation," with access to the newest technologies, and ample financial resources, configuring the telecommunications corporation of the 21st century to: (1) offer a package of long-distance, local exchange, and data services, (2) outside of FCC and state regulatory jurisdiction. This can be realized by reorganizing from the ground up as a CLEC, separating the delivery of services from the ownership and operation of the local wireline loop. One already observes the ILECs attempting to mutate in this direction through their applications under section 706 of the Telecommunications Act of 1996, in which they propose to exempt new generations of data services from the unbundling requirements for local telephony under sections 251 and 252 of the act. But the narrow possibility of a managerial plus technological salvation should not deflect attention from the billions of dollars wasted in seeking to overcome regulatory barriers to achieve strategies that enhance the growth of the industry. Clearly, whether evasion is worth the costs is a question that must be asked also by every nation now establishing a body of telecommunications regulation like that in America. Regulators in other nations who look to the American experience for guidance should therefore heed the Latin maxim, *Caveat emptor*.

INDEX

MIX
Papier aus verantwortungsvollen Quellen
Paper from responsible sources
FSC® C105338

If you have any concerns about our products,
you can contact us on
ProductSafety@springernature.com

In case Publisher is established outside the EU,
the EU authorized representative is:
Springer Nature Customer Service Center GmbH
Europaplatz 3, 69115 Heidelberg, Germany

Printed by Libri Plureos GmbH
in Hamburg, Germany